# Over-Tested and Under-Prepared

Pressured by standardized testing and rigid pacing guidelines, many schools are forced to cover too much content too quickly, without being able to meet the needs of individual students. In this powerful book from acclaimed author and presenter Bob Sornson, you'll learn how shifting from curriculum-based instruction to competency based, personalized learning can help students become more successful, confident, and engaged learners.

Each chapter is easy to digest and provides compelling research, strategies, and anecdotes to inspire conversation and action. This second edition provides updated statistics and examples of schools successfully using competency based learning models to help you bring about meaningful change.

Teachers, administrators, and community leaders will all find practical resources and a clear rationale for transforming our current educational system into a new, dynamic model of teaching and learning.

**Bob Sornson** is the founder of the Early Learning Foundation. For more than three decades he was a classroom teacher and school administrator, and he's the author of many books and articles for educators, parents, and children. He works with schools and education organizations across the country, focusing primarily on developing whole-child competency-based programs that support early learning success.

# Also Available from Routledge Eye On Education
(www.routledge.com/k-12)

**Questioning Education: Moving from What and How to Why and Who**
Sean Slade

**Flip the System US: How Teachers Can Transform Education and Save Democracy**
Michael Soskil

**Students Taking Charge in Grades K-5: Inside the Learner-Active, Technology-Infused Classroom**
Nancy Sulla

**Students Taking Charge in Grades 6-12: Inside the Learner-Active, Technology-Infused Classroom**
Nancy Sulla

**Students Taking Charge Implementation Guide for Leaders: Inside the Learner-Active, Technology-Infused Classroom**
Nancy Sulla

# Over-Tested and Under-Prepared

Shifting from One-Size-Fits-All Instruction to Personalized Competency Based Learning

Second Edition

Bob Sornson

NEW YORK AND LONDON

Cover image: © Thinkstock

Second edition published 2023
by Routledge
605 Third Avenue, New York, NY 10158

and by Routledge
4 Park Square, Milton Park, Abingdon, Oxon, OX14 4RN

*Routledge is an imprint of the Taylor & Francis Group, an informa business*

© 2023 Taylor & Francis

The right of Bob Sornson to be identified as author of this work has been asserted in accordance with sections 77 and 78 of the Copyright, Designs and Patents Act 1988.

All rights reserved. No part of this book may be reprinted or reproduced or utilised in any form or by any electronic, mechanical, or other means, now known or hereafter invented, including photocopying and recording, or in any information storage or retrieval system, without permission in writing from the publishers.

*Trademark notice*: Product or corporate names may be trademarks or registered trademarks, and are used only for identification and explanation without intent to infringe.

First edition published by Routledge 2016

ISBN: 978-1-032-26698-5 (hbk)
ISBN: 978-1-032-25462-3 (pbk)
ISBN: 978-1-003-28952-4 (ebk)

DOI: 10.4324/9781003289524

Typeset in Palatino
by MPS Limited, Dehradun

To those stubborn educators who have held to their beliefs that education can be a joyous and collaborative process.

To every parent who wants your children to fall in love with learning, and also wants all children to have a fair opportunity to learn and succeed.

To every child. May you be blessed with determined adults who will help you fall in love with learning for life.

# Contents

*About the Author* .................................... ix
*Acknowledgements*..................................... x
*Reader's Guide* ..................................... xii

**Introduction** ...................................... 1

1 **Someday Soon, a Fable** ........................... 5

2 **Informed Instruction Leads to Competency, Part One** ............................................ 10

3 **The Curriculum-Driven Model: A Brief History** ....... 15

4 **Without Learning Competency There Can Be No Equity** .......................................... 34

5 **Giving Up Unproductive Mental Models** ............ 39

6 **Building a New Model** ............................ 49

7 **Principles of Instruction Leading to Competency** ..... 57

8 **Teaching Differently** ............................. 62

9 **Systems Thinking for Competency Based Learning** ........................................... 72

10 **Whole Child Competency** ......................... 93

11 **Creating the Culture of a Learning Organization** ..... 101

12 Learning for Understanding and Application ........ 109

13 Masters of the Trade: Game Designers .............. 117

14 What's Happening in Competency Based
   Learning Initiatives ................................. 121

15 Teacher Education: Building Pathways to
   Skills That Matter................................... 150

16 Distracted by the Debate Over What to Cover ....... 159

17 Letting Go of Curriculum-Driven Instruction ........ 161

18 Transitioning from Curriculum-Driven to
   Competency Based Learning ........................ 168

19 Informed Instruction Leads to Competency,
   Part Two............................................. 174

20 Conclusion: The Spirit of Transformation ........... 177

   *Appendix 1: Organizational Self-Assessment for Readiness
              to Implement Competency Based Learning* ....181
   *Appendix 2: Resources for the Further Study of
              Competency Based Learning* ................182
   *Study Guide* ...........................................187
   *References* ............................................198

# About the Author

**Bob Sornson** is an education leader calling for programs and practices which support competency based learning, early learning success, and high quality early childhood learning programs. He is the father of four grown children, and has worked internationally with school districts, universities, and parent organizations.

Born and raised in Detroit, MI along with his six siblings, Bob earned a bachelor's and master's degree at the University of Michigan, an education specialist degree from Central Michigan University, and his PH.D. from Andrews University. For over thirty years he worked as a teacher and as an administrator in Michigan public schools, developed an acclaimed model early learning success initiative, and in 2001 founded the **Early Learning Foundation.**

A prolific author, Bob has written best-selling books for educators, parents and children, along with many journal publications. His books include *Essential Math Skills* (Shell Education), *Fanatically Formative* (Corwin Press), *Stand in My Shoes: Kids Learning about Empathy* (Early Learning Foundation Press), *The Juice Box Bully* (Early Learning Foundation Press), *Teaching and Joy* (ASCD). He has offered workshops and keynotes in forty-eight states and in other nations.

**Bob Sornson** is dedicated to giving far more children a real chance for success in school and in life, and believes that the task of helping all kids become avid learners is one of the great challenges/opportunities of our time. Bob lives with his wife Nancy in Brighton, MI, and can be contacted at earlylearningfoundation.com.

# Acknowledgements

After four decades of "school reform", the disappointing implementation and results of No Child Left Behind, the thinly disguised federalization of schools that was Race to the Top, and the learning losses imposed during the Covid pandemic years, **the American public has become disheartened.** The public questions whether education leaders and our government have the capacity to thoughtfully consider and implement a plan for the meaningful improvement of our system of education. Many educators are discouraged.

Principals and teachers wonder where the joy went. Young men and women with the capacity to be extraordinary teachers have taken a different career path.

And yet, everywhere across this nation there are educators, parents, and community leaders who still have that spark in their eyes, holding onto a vision of learning systems that effectively serve students of every race and level of affluence, giving our children a real chance to compete in the global society, inspiring a love of learning that can last a lifetime. This book is for you.

This book was first published in 2016, and since then the interest in competency based learning has grown exponentially. But implementation has lagged behind interest. We publish this updated edition to bring as many practical ideas for application as possible to those who are working to create meaningful change, along with the updated research to support the why's and how's of this transformation toward schools that help far more kids become lifelong learners.

To my great fortune, I get to meet and work with people who believe in their hearts and souls that we can build educational systems and institutions which truly serve our students, respecting their differences and honoring their strengths.

They are not deterred from effective action by political drama and smothering bureaucracies. They are committed to building a better world for our children, and schools that work is part of that vision. They are found from Mississippi to Michigan, from California to Maine, and in nations around the world. They inspire me.

I am especially grateful to the following people who made this book possible:

To Lauren Davis, my editor at Routledge, who from the first day she received my book proposal, understood the message and believed there is an audience, and whose enthusiasm for this work moved it forward with astonishing positive energy.

To Casey Reason and Jim Scott, who share my tribulations and never ever advise me to play it safe.

To Rebecca, Matt, Alicia, and Molly, whose lives inspire my belief that ideas can make a difference.

To Nancy, who walks the path with me, whose kindness and decency surrounds every project and every day.

# Reader's Guide

This book describes a model of learning unlike the one most of us experienced as students. It is my hope that readers who understand the concepts and research in this book will embrace the belief that improved systems for learning are possible. Instead of responding with all the reasons why change is hard, it is my hope that many of you will see a role for yourself as we begin the creation of a new way of learning that allows for every child to access a path to becoming a lifelong learner.

The first portion of *Over-tested and Under-prepared* begins with a look at what's possible, just enough to fill your heart with hope. Then we look back at the design of the education model we've used in schools for well more than a hundred years, with an eye for understanding why it was built as it is. By understanding the basic architecture of our system we can more fully understand why it no longer serves the vast majority of students. Then we'll dig deeply into a new way of thinking about learning, in school and in life. In the final chapters we consider the steps you might take to lead the transformation in your school or community.

**My hope is that this book rekindles your belief that real education systems change is possible,** that we can elevate learning outcomes for all kids, especially those who are vulnerable to the vagaries of our present system for covering content in a joyless one-size-fits-all race. As part of that systems change, our schools must once again become trusted by parents, respected by the community, and be a place where educators thrive within a culture that challenges us while also giving us real tools to help kids succeed. Thank you for joining us on this pathway to change.

Educators, parents, students, and community leaders can study this text with many varied purposes, perhaps including the following:

- Read and share. Create a new vision for schools and learning which better serves students, parents, communities, and employers. Become an idea leader in your community.
- Read with the purpose of gathering resources or specific ideas for the transformation you already want to occur.
- Create personal or professional learning communities, using this book as a catalyst to dialog and collaboration toward the creation of new learning systems.
- Identify crucial learning outcomes for yourself or your organization, and use the many resources in this book to help you design a plan for sustained learning.
- Develop a leadership team, to transform your schools or to build synergy between learning organizations, and build your transformation plan with the insights of those who have already travelled this path.

# Introduction

**With only a month remaining in the school year, a young high school biology teacher** is confronted with an unpleasant challenge. There are three more chapters to cover, but not nearly enough time to teach or cover all their content. He's teaching an honors class, but for the past several months he's been struggling to manage behavior and keep his students on-task. Many of them are frustrated and struggling to understand the material. Some have already disengaged from the learning process, having decided that science is too hard, not fun, and incredibly boring.

Three more chapters, with content including Population Ecology, Behavioral Biology, Community Biology, Ecosystems and Conservation Biology. All the other Bio teachers are on-track to finish every chapter in the text, and the district clearly expects him to cover all this content. So this young, hopeful, and idealistic young teacher will set aside good teaching and rush through the remaining chapters with students who are already disinterested or disconnected.

**Half-way through the year, a third grade teacher** prepares to move on to the next math lesson. She's been teaching for many years, but it is getting harder. The pressure of the state assessment looms. Looking around her classroom, she can easily identify which students love math. There are only a few. The others don't get it. The math program moves so quickly through the material. It feels like a race.

Her district has adopted a math program that allows no room for variance. Everyone gets the same lesson on the same day. Some of the kids lack basic number sense. Many of them have memorized facts and formulas, but do not fully comprehend why these rules apply. Spiraling, they told her. Don't slow down. In a few months the expertly designed math curriculum will spiral around and cover the same material, so if students don't understand basic concepts now, just keep going. Teaching math used to be fun, but not anymore.

**It's the beginning of the year. A sixth grade teacher considers her new class**, goofy adolescents vying for attention and respect, searching for social connection, hoping for safety and status. But in her hands is the pacing guide, the guide for what must be taught, how quickly, and in what sequence.

She looks at her beautiful students. Every impulse in her begs to get to know them, build relationships with them. She wants to build a positive classroom culture, help them get to know each other, set standards for how we treat others and want to be treated. She would like to assess their learning needs, figure out each child's strengths. She would like to find out their special interests, the things that might motivate them to work a little harder. But she cannot.

In response to diminished outcomes on the state test, her district has adopted a more rigorous curriculum, a pacing guide for every subject, and biweekly assessments. Each day she is required to write the code for the CCSS standards which are being addressed by today's lessons on the whiteboard. If an administrator comes into the classroom and finds that she is not focused on those standards, she could be reprimanded.

Scanning her classroom, she sees the students who are nervous and socially awkward. She pauses, makes eye contact with each of them, and smiles. She notices the kids who are wiggly, who need movement and lots of practice learning to be calm and self-regulated. Then glancing at the pacing guide, she forges ahead. Ready or not, here it comes.

**In the 21st century, good teachers are being asked** to use the supercharged version of a curriculum-driven instructional model that treats kids as if they were learning on an assembly line. Covering way too much content at an unreasonable rate, with rigid pacing guides that make it impossible to find time to shape instruction to meet the individual needs of students, the system is breaking down. In spite of teaching to the test, our children are not doing better on international comparisons or compared to previous decades. Good teachers are discouraged.

Many of the best and brightest college students cannot imagine subjecting themselves to working in such a broken system. State and national legislators fiddle mindlessly with our schools, adding layers of regulation that confuse and befuddle both educators and parents. In the information age, an era in which learning skills and the desire to learn have never been more important, many capable students are not developing the skills needed to achieve economic and personal success.

**In this book, we will explore simple ideas** that will help teacher-leaders, administrators, and parents create learning systems in which both educators and students have a much better chance to succeed. **The steps are simple. Identify crucial learning outcomes. Teach and practice crucial learning outcomes for as long as it takes to develop competency. Design instruction for crucial outcomes in a student's zone of proximal development. Learn to track the progress of each student along the pathways to crucial outcomes. Include students in the planning process for developing advanced-level learning plans. Deliver instruction and monitor progress in all the domains of development which contribute to a life of learning and success.**

**Beginning with the end in mind,** we will reflect on a new vision for our schools, along with strategies to convert an obsolete system into a dynamic model of teaching and learning. We will carefully consider the history of how our present system was developed, not to criticize but to understand. Then we will look at the learning and implementation challenges we may face at every level of instruction, and consider steps forward. Change is challenging. Transformation is possible. And this is the time for both in our schools.

**Most educators who works in our schools** are among the most dedicated and compassionate people in the world. The students who come to our schools need us to do better, not by adding more pressure to our existing structure, but by reconceptualizing our system to meet the needs of modern learners. Learning outcomes have never been more important. This book suggests a change in the underlying architecture of our design for education that will allow us to make teaching an honor and pleasure, and to help students fall in love with learning for life.

**We are at the inception of the most exciting time in the history of education.** For those who are ready to innovate, the opportunities to lead and create are endless. We have barely scratched the surface of the potential for human learning. Decades of discovery and transformation lie ahead, and some of you reading this book will likely lead the way. From the ashes of decades of failed school reform you will construct education systems that bring learning alive for our children, offer the most effective antidote to poverty, bring respect and collegiality back to the profession of teaching, and create a more productive and peaceful world for all our children.

# 1

# Someday Soon, a Fable

When it was time for Matt to go to preschool we picked a school with a great reputation, a calm and thoughtful school culture, and some really good teachers. But even though we believed we had chosen well, we were surprised when they showed us their system for tracking progress toward important early childhood competencies. These outcomes included all aspects of development, and we knew they'd be paying careful attention to oral language, sensory-motor, social, behavior, and self-regulation, and self-care skills along with early literacy and numeracy skills. The teachers promised to keep track of his skill development so they'd never overlook something crucial, and they would know how to challenge him enough but never too much. It amazed us how well they knew our boy, and how we were included in the planning process and able to learn more about what to do with our son at home.

By the time he was old enough for Kindergarten, he had exceeded the standard for competency in several of the domains of early childhood, he loved school, and he loved learning. It was hard to leave that preschool, but they helped us find an elementary program that picked right up where they had left off.

The elementary school took Matt's inventory of competent skills and knew right where to focus on his learning needs and strengths. By the middle of his Kindergarten year, he was happily working on first grade math. Self-regulation skills took a little longer to reach proficiency, and his hand-eye skills needed some extra practice time, but the teacher knew his ability levels and gave him exactly what he needed. It was like that all through the early grades. Sometimes he joined kids from another grade for reading and math groups.

Amazingly these teachers never seemed rushed. We worried about that, since many of the schools we'd visited seemed to be highly stressed environments in which teachers raced through their lessons and never let kids play. But in Matt's school it wasn't like that. There was time for activities, projects, music, nature, and art. The teachers had well-established routines that included time for talking, play, art, and developing social skills.

We wondered sometimes, and once we asked the teacher if they should be pushing Matt harder. She smiled like she'd heard that question many times before. Then she explained that by knowing her students well, she could give them just enough challenge without pushing kids into the frustration zone. It made sense, and she showed us the school's test scores. Pushing kids beyond their abilities makes kids shut down. In addition to better test scores in the short run, she explained, the work they were doing was more likely to help Matt love math, love reading and writing, and love learning for the rest of his life.

By Matt's fourth grade year he had a solid learning foundation, and the school had developed a profile of his skills. They showed us the learning steps that lead to competency or competency in mathematics, technology, social science, reading, writing, cultural awareness, personal health, social-emotional development, career development, service learning, arts and science.

Kids could take all the time and get all the support needed to become proficient at every step along the pathways to competency. Even kids from less fortunate backgrounds flourished in this school. All they needed was a chance.

From that point forward Matt had a personalized learning plan that considered his interests and needs, the recommendations of his teachers, and the things we thought were most important for our son. Science was broken up into modules, and he didn't just learn so he could pass a test; he learned so he could really understand. There were no grades. It was all about deep understanding, and he could take as much time as needed to develop a new technology skill, math skill, or learn a new form of writing.

At some point during the middle school years Matt discovered the microbiome. Something about the balance of bacteria and other critters living in the gut fascinated him. So his teachers found lots of ways to incorporate learning about the microbiome into his math, science, geography, writing, and reading activities. It was exciting watching his learning profile as he progressed along the pathways to competency. There were so many options for learning. At school there were modules of instruction, lots of mini-courses for enrichment or exploration, community and nature projects, sports and extracurricular activities, and even internships. There were online learning options for both home and school. Community members were brought in to be instructors for special topics.

During all those years I never once heard Matt or his friends talk about wanting to find an easy course or an easy teacher. The whole concept of wanting to get a good grade without having to give much effort was gone from the schools. Learning was for a purpose, and there was no such thing as pretend-competency. You were competent when you had the knowledge and skills and could apply them in complex ways. Or you weren't. Occasionally Matt would slack off a bit, but slackers did not gain new skills and he saw that and quickly around.

By the time he got to high school Matt was already close to meeting the standards for graduation in a couple of the domains of learning. He was able to extend his learning through volunteer work in the community, and by taking on a couple of apprenticeships. For the students in this high school, learning was a mix of modules taught at school, blended learning modules, apprenticeship and internships, project based learning, community college technical programs, and international cohort groups for special projects.

Because of the personalized learning plans and the competency profiles, the line between high school and post-secondary education was pretty blurred. Some of his classes were at the community college, and others were in the basement of one of the technology companies in our town.

For us as parents, one of the greatest joys was watching him take charge of his own learning. Sure there were minimum competencies he had to reach, but Matt got to choose the skills for which he wanted to achieve something better than competency. There were so many paths to competency, and beyond competency. He was able to find the areas of knowledge and skill that fascinated him, and so his interested in learning continued to grow. By the time he graduated high school there were no more GPAs at his school. That was considered an antiquated concept from another age. In addition to a high school diploma, he'd earned competencies and certificates from the community college and from one of our state universities.

The high schools, community colleges, state and private universities had worked out a system of verified competencies and shared learning pathways. Degrees and certificates no longer measured seat time and credits, but instead reflected whether a student had the skills, knowledge, and application represented by a specific degree. You could finish a program in six months or three years, and finishing meant something.

Matt has advanced certificates and degrees now, but he's not done learning. Some of his learning is facilitated by one of the universities, but often it's the product of a network of professionals our son has come to know from around the world. It's all about learning, he says. Sometimes he teaches a module at the middle or high school. He really likes that. In his own work he does research, and often collaborates with one of the local hospitals.

We have two grandchildren now and another on the way. These kids will never be forced to endure the old curriculum-driven, one-size-fits-all, seat time, and Carnegie credit system. They'll never be rewarded with a good grade for picking an easy teacher or a blow off class. Our grandkids will recognize that we all learn differently, in our own way and at our own pace. They will understand that learning is too precious to consider making kids race through content they don't understand, memorize facts and protocols to pass a test, or to make a child sit through months of boring lessons they already understand.

Our grandchildren will see learning as a beautiful challenge, a privilege, and a lifelong pursuit. From the preschool that carefully builds the foundation of learning, to the years in which they discover their own special interests, to the years in which they extend knowledge and collaborate with learners around the globe, these children will walk the pathways to competency.

(Note: This story is a fable. Someday it will be the true story of the learning lives of many children).

# 2

# Informed Instruction Leads to Competency, Part One

Careful observation, followed by an informed choice of instruction that fits the needs of the individual students, watchful monitoring of progress toward essential outcomes, and then more choices about how to encourage, teach, or intervene for our kids; that is informed instruction.

- With a toddler learning to walk, we hold her hand. We check the surroundings for safety, and then let go at just the right time to watch her step forward on her own.
- With a child learning to throw and catch, we assess his skills, decide whether to use the beanbag or a larger playground ball, and then throw carefully so that the ball is easily catchable.
- We carefully consider our choice of a book for an early reader. Then we sit close and practice reading, carefully observing whether the experience of reading this book is interesting, highly successful, and fun. Hopefully the chosen book is a good match, but if it isn't we change plans and find another book.

Informed instruction is our best attempt to give kids what they need at their level of readiness. A good coach knows the skills of her players, and designs practice activities that are challenging but never so difficult that the kids get frustrated and quit trying. A teenager learning to drive gets up early on a Sunday morning. Dad drives with him to the high school parking lot. No one is there. The lot is empty. No cars to hit. No distractions. This is an opportunity to safely practice beginning driving skills. Thoughtful parents don't take their teenager out to drive on the highway until he is fully prepared to be successful.

Informed instruction includes the identification of all the steps needed to reach our goal. When teaching a child to build and fly a kite, we plan the steps carefully. We lay out the paper together, and then cautiously attach it to the frame of the kite, making every inch secure. We attach the string and tail, giving the child as much independence as possible, but checking each step and suggesting changes as needed. Once outside we show our kids how to check the wind, and consider in which direction we should lay out the kite. We check for power lines and other obstacles. And only then it is time to learn to run into the face of the wind and watch the kite rise far above us.

> **Crucial instruction does not take shortcuts. Competency is competency. When teaching our kids to ride a bike, we carefully judge their readiness and then offer sufficient instruction and practice every step of the way.**

When the outcomes are really important, we find ways to use informed instruction, which leads to competency. When training a pilot to fly, we ensure that there is sufficient training, practice, and many demonstrations of competency before he is allowed to fly alone or with passengers. When you hire a master electrician you know they have had a supervised training program, served as an apprentice, and demonstrated competency is every essential skill.

Medical doctors do not complete their training by taking a class in which they receive an overview of surgery, or an introduction to the use of medications. Covering content is not enough to ensure learning or competence. In any general or specialty area of practice, they are expected to demonstrate that they have both the knowledge and the skills. The crucial medical knowledge and skills are clearly delineated.

Most of our Pre-K to Grade 12 schools, unfortunately, are not models of informed instruction leading to competency. For more than a century we have used a curriculum-driven model of instruction that includes long lists of content to cover in each grade, and in recent years has added the pressure of high-stakes standardized assessment. We use rigid pacing guides that require teachers to stay up with the expected rate of coverage. Some schools use scripted learning programs, which demand that every child receives the same instruction at the same time. We expect teachers to cover more content than humanly possible, and we expect all kids to keep up.

If we used a rigidly paced system like ours while building a house, the results would not be pretty. With a timetable that doesn't allow for sick workers or bad weather, the foundation would not yet be complete when it is time to begin working on the frame. Because the foundation is unfinished and uneven, building the frame gets more complicated. When it is time to put on the drywall, the frame is sloppy and the plumbing and electrical are unfinished. But a timetable is a timetable, and the workers are required to move forward, and stay on schedule.

The plumbing leaks and the electrical system does not work; the drywall is uneven and unpainted. But it is time for the house to go on sale. How long would this construction company stay in business?

**Some learning outcomes are crucial.** These deserve careful assessment of student readiness, informed instruction at the student's instructional level, and all the time, instruction and intervention needed for the development of complete competency. Another way of expressing this: **Take your time with the important stuff.**

We all know that early learning success is crucial to long-term learning success, and key skills in the development of language, literacy, numeracy, motor skills, and behavior and self-regulation skills deserve the support needed to achieve competency. But in spite of a near universal acceptance of the importance of early learning success, we continue to use a curriculum-driven and pacing guide-driven system of instruction in most schools.

Crucial oral language skills, literacy skills, and phonological skills can be identified as necessary building blocks for helping a child become a proficient reader, but in our one-size-fits-all instructional system, a majority of children do not fully achieve the skills needed to become proficient readers by third grade.

In math, there are key skills which build the foundation of number sense that is needed to understand and enjoy math for life. Behavior and self-regulation skills are as important as any academic skill in predicting long-term learning success, but are not tested on any state or national standardized assessment. None the less, they are crucial and deserve to be developed to competency.

> **This book examines the basic model of instruction we've used for more than a century, and finds it lacking. Rather than asking teachers to teach more or teach faster, we seek ways to work smarter. We want a system that works far better for our students, while also creating a system that supports teacher success and attracts many of the best and brightest adults to want to work in the schools.**

We seek better learning outcomes for our students, so that many more students can have the skills and behaviors to be successful lifelong learners in the information age. This requires a love of learning based on successful learning experiences, and also the competent skills needed to move forward to learning outcomes that allow us to live socially and financially flourishing lives.

The divide between the rich and the poor is growing in our country. **This growing disparity is in part based on family affluence and opportunity. But much of it is based on the gap in learning competencies**.

In the early childhood years, high-quality oral language skills, literacy, numeracy, and motor skills matter. Self-regulation, the ability to self-calm, focus, persist, delay gratification, and adjust your mood and behavior to meet the situation, matters.

Racing through content has not/does not/and will not give us better outcomes. We've tried. Racing through content has damaged countless young learners. We have a responsibility to help children develop a deep love of learning, a positive association between reading, thinking, problem-solving, math, science, and learning by the end of third grade. In this we have utterly failed, and its time to do so much better.

As students get older, literacy and math matter, but so do other crucial aspects of learning. Competent skills for scientific thinking and self-directed learning matter. Technology skills matter. Social skills matter. Within our present system, some of these content areas are included in the curriculum, and therefore "covered." But coverage does not imply deep learning, nor the development of skills that will matter to a person's life.

Competency based learning and informed instruction are not new concepts. We use these concepts at home every day as we raise our children. We use them in education institutions that serve professions in which competence is perceived as crucial. And now it is time to build systems of learning for all our children that are based on personalized competency based learning.

> **In this world of opportunity, competency is the primary antidote to poverty.**

Today, learning success is crucial for all our children. No longer can we afford to rely on a system which is designed for only a small percentage to become highly skilled learners. Our children and our professional educators deserve a thoughtful learning model that helps every child develop at his/her own pace toward crucial learning outcomes. Without a system for learning that respects individual differences, builds skills one step at a time, and allows both affluent and poor kids to become self-motivated lifelong learners, we will continue to produce the same unacceptable results we have been producing for the last several decades.

# 3

# The Curriculum-Driven Model: A Brief History

## A Model Built for the 19th and Early 20th Centuries

The systems design for American public schools was significantly influenced by the work of Horace Mann and Frederick Winslow Taylor. Mann was the Secretary of the first Massachusetts State Board Of Education. In 1843 he travelled to Europe to study the education systems of the time, and after his return supported the adoption of the Prussian education system, which became the adopted system in Massachusetts, then New York, and eventually the other states. The Prussian system provided an eight-year course of primary education and emphasized the skills needed in an early industrialized world (reading, writing, and arithmetic) along with education in ethics, duty, discipline, and obedience. Affluent children often went on to attend preparatory private schools for an additional four years, but most children did not advance beyond eighth grade (Downs, 1974; Taylor, 2010).

Mann was also the founder of the *Common School Journal*, in which he offered six main principles for public education:

- ♦ The public should no longer remain ignorant.

- Public education should be paid for, controlled, and sustained by an interested public.
- Public education will be best provided in schools that embrace children from a variety of backgrounds.
- Public education must be non-sectarian (https://en.wikipedia.org/wiki/Nonsectarian).
- Education must be taught by the spirit, methods, and discipline of a free society (https://en.wikipedia.org/wiki/Free_society).
- Education should be provided by well-trained, professional teachers.

Frederick Winslow Taylor was an American inventor and engineer who developed a set of management principles in which waste is avoided and production is improved, called scientific management theory. His efficiency principles are described in his book *The Principles of Scientific Management* (1911).

He studied the motions required to complete a task, devised a way to break the task down into component motions, and looked for the most efficient and effective manner to do the work. This was described as "the one best way." Taylor recommended enforced standardization of methods, a clear distinction between management and workers, and strong management control (Kanigel, 1997).

The influence of Taylor is seen in the organization and management of schools in the early parts of the 20th century. The development of curriculum, grade level learning material, and standard delivery of instruction reflect the philosophy of Taylor. Students were organized into classrooms by grades, in spite of what we see today as significant variance among the learning readiness of same-age students. Instruction was organized into subject areas, separating social studies from reading, math from science. Standard units of time (class periods) were used to separate subject areas and give the same time to each subject. Teachers were separated into classrooms designed for teacher-directed coverage of grade level curricula. The distinction between teaching staff and administration was clearly delineated and reinforced by pay, power, and prestige.

Taylor's influence on the design of our schools has persisted over time. We still separate kids by grade, cover standardized curricula by subject matter, create pacing guides to keep teachers on track, offer credits by measuring seat time, and confer graduation diplomas, which measure the number of credits rather than the learning skills of our students. Students are subjected to "the one best way" of standardized instruction, which is incredibly boring for some students and frustrating and impossible for others.

Google, Intel, Starbucks, Quicken, Salesforce, Clearbit, Apple, and most modern businesses have long ago rejected the strict standardization of Taylor's methodology. Collaboration, continuous learning, and innovation are the canons of modern business. Modern businesses must learn and adapt to survive. They recognize the acceleration of learning when teams of people collaborate. They recognize the importance of business culture and a sense of community on the effectiveness of their employees.

**Today's mantra in a thriving business is learn, adapt, experiment, and improve within a culture that encourages respect and collaboration. Public schools have continued to use the "one best way" of standardized delivery of grade level content objectives, with little professional collaboration or innovation.**

Mann promoted public education for all using the Prussian teacher-directed and grade-based model. Taylor sought to add efficiency by standardizing instruction by age/grade, subject matter, separation of classrooms, and by establishing a clear distinction between the influence and authority of teachers and administration. In this system, learning is measured by seat time and credits earned, **and instruction is delivered in the same way to all students.**

In schools, we continue to use a 100-plus-year-old systems model, which most successful modern businesses have abandoned.

## Our Society Has Changed, but not Our Schools

In 1900, the rate of graduation from high school in the United States was 6.4%. By 1910 it had risen slightly to 8.8% (EPE Research Center, 2010; US Census Bureau, 2014). For most folks, primary-level education was enough. The advantages of advanced levels of learning were not enough to motivate large numbers of students and their families to make the choice to stay in school. A strong back and a good work ethic were enough for the demands of most jobs.

> **In the context of the early 1900s public education existed comfortably with the cover and sort methods that are part of the curriculum-driven model. With a vast majority of students not going beyond eighth grade, and with jobs not dependent on advanced learning skills, there was no pressure for all students to succeed in school. High rates of literacy and mathematical skill were not required in the workplace.**

Taylor's principles of efficiency worked well enough within the needs of the early 1900s. The development of a standard curriculum, grade level learning material, and pacing expectations for each course went unquestioned, even as large numbers of students were uninspired and unsuccessful in the classroom. With the influence of Thorndike and others, the use of testing also became a greater part of the educational model.

In the economic and social context of the early 1900s, as public education and compulsory schooling were still developing, the use of a standardized curriculum and testing system made sense. Students were exposed to content without any serious commitment to helping all students become highly successful or lifelong learners. The use of a one-size-fits-all model left many students behind because of developmental differences, experience differences, and language differences, but it did not matter to society as long as many jobs did not require higher levels of learning skill.

> **Sorting students into bluebirds and blackbirds may have been hurtful to individual students, but in the early 1900s society had plenty of room for blackbirds.**

After World War II, industrial innovation and the development of new technologies began to change the face of business. Interest in improved learning outcomes increased, and high school graduation and college entry rates began to rise significantly. Many more people saw education as important for their own lives and for the lives of their children.

But **as the perceived importance of education increased, we held onto our familiar model of instruction:** Efficient delivery of a standard curriculum. Using the same old design for instruction, **we responded to the pressure for better outcomes by speeding up the assembly line.**

In response to the need for greater learning and technical skills in the workplace there were many calls for improved learning outcomes in our schools. We added more content, much more. Teachers were expected to cover more content in the same time allotted. We shifted some of this content to younger age-range delivery, which meant that content once delivered in fourth grade might now be covered in second grade. Gradually, beginning in the 1970s, and then with a rush in the late 1980s, we began to add testing systems to hold teachers and schools accountable. Our use of the curriculum-driven model was never seriously questioned during these decades.

> **As the importance of literacy, math, science, technology, problem-solving, and the ability to continue learning throughout life increased, we held onto our familiar model of standardized delivery of instruction. We cover curricula, we test students, then we assign grades and move forward to the next unit or lesson.**

As job requirements became more complex, business leaders continued to call for improvements in public education. Public attention to the results of international testing data added even more pressure on our schools, as American children fell conspicuously behind other nations. Politicians joined into the fray, imposing additional reporting and testing requirements. National data showed discrepancies among racial subgroups and between the affluent and the poor, and more pressure came to bear. We've federalized the assessment systems, adopted national standards for curriculum, and imposed evaluation structures in which teachers are judged by student test scores.

In 1983, the President's Commission on Excellence in Education published its report, *A Nation at Risk: The Imperative for Educational Reform*. The report famously stated, **"The educational foundations of our society are presently being eroded by a rising tide of mediocrity that threatens our very future as a Nation and a people. If an unfriendly foreign power had attempted to impose on America the mediocre educational performance that exists today, we might well have viewed it as an act of war."** The report supported the idea that American schools were failing and touched off a wave of state and federal reform efforts, which continue to this day.

In 1989, President George H.W. Bush convened a summit with governors, business leaders, and key political advisors in Charlottesville, VA, for the first ever National Education Summit. Bill Clinton (Arkansas), Roy Romer (Colorado), and Terry Branstad (Iowa) were key leaders among the governors. **No educators were invited to this summit, which laid the foundation for federal education policy for years to come.**

The 1989 Summit led to Goals 2000: Educate America Act (March 1994), which famously promised that by the year 2000, every child would start school ready to learn, the high school graduation rate would reach 90%, U.S. students would be first in the world in science and mathematics, every American adult would be literate, every school free of drugs and violence, and every school would promote partnerships with parents.

In the public discourse, there were strong demands to improve our education outcomes, and promises were made. During subsequent years we have seen the No Child Left Behind Act (2002), Race to the Top (2009), implementation of

Common Core State Standards (2010), and Every Student Succeeds Act (2015). But throughout this age of politically guided school reform, we have held firmly to the **Cover Test and Sort delivery model.** We have increased pressure to "cover" the entirety of the curriculum so that student would be ready for mandated standardized tests. The pressure to cover and test has been codified into state and federal regulations.

The need and the demand to improve learning outcomes in our schools have been building for decades, and yet we still operate within the basic systems design of Horace Mann and Frederick Winslow Taylor, a system that prioritizes efficient delivery and testing of a standard curriculum. We cover, we test, and we move on. Students are sorted by whether they keep up with the curriculum. We deliver more content, and we deliver it faster, and we test it more rigorously, but it is the same basic system design we've used for more than a hundred and fifty years.

## Consistently Failing to Serve the Needs of Our Society and Students

For many years high levels of skill in math, science, and reading were arguably crucial for only a privileged few. Our Mann-Taylor designed curriculum-driven system successfully sorted out the less fortunate, motivated, or talented learners with no ill effects on society. A small group of educated men and women was enough. The education model based on coverage, grading, and sorting worked well enough to meet our needs.

**But the learning needs of our society are no longer well-served by this model.** We are living in an age of ideas and innovation. To live successfully within modern society, people need to learn, develop skills and knowledge, and then continue to learn so they can keep up with the pace of change and avoid irrelevance in the workplace. The requirements of medium and high wage jobs include math, reading, technical skills, problem-solving skills, collaboration skills, and the capacity to continue to learn and keep up with new information and technical advances.

Being a successful learner, and developing the capacity for intrinsically motivated learning, has never been more crucial for the financial and social future of individual students. **Becoming a nation in which most students are successful learners has never been more important to the economic future of our society.** And yet, the system of education we rely upon has failed to give us the better outcomes we need for the benefit of our economy and our citizens, especially our most vulnerable citizens.

> **The cover test and sort (CTS) instructional delivery system of a hundred years ago, even in its present juiced-up form, is not producing outcomes which are good for society, good for individuals, or fair to students with fewer advantages at home.**

The importance of learning is reflected in the improved rates of high school graduation over the last decade. In 2014, about 79% of all public high school students graduated on time, and about 70% of economically disadvantaged students graduated on time (NCES, 2014). By the school year 2018–19, the national adjusted cohort graduation rate (ACGR) for public high school students was 85.8%, the highest recorded rate since beginning to collect this data in 2010–11. Asian/Pacific Islander students had the highest ACGR (93%), followed by White (89%), Hispanic (82%), Black (80%), and American Indian/Alaska Native (74%) students. (National Center for Education Statistics, 2020).

**But graduation in itself does not guarantee that students have the skills for lifelong learning.** Among 12th grade students (remember that a significant group of students has already dropped out by this point), **only 24% score at or above proficient levels in math, and only 37% are proficient or better in reading.**

Students who manage to graduate from high school but do not have proficient skills face great challenges in college or technical training and even greater challenges in the workplace. This has long been a special challenge for minority children in the U.S. **Among students tested on the NAEP,**

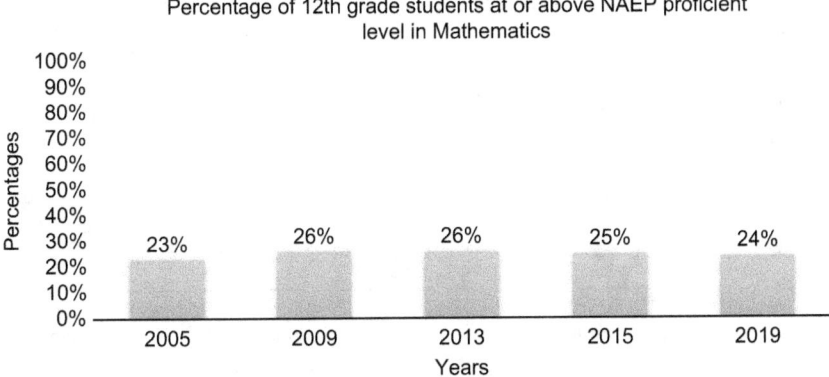

**FIGURE 3.1** Trends in twelfth-grade NAEP mathematics achievement-level results
Source: NAEP Mathematics: National Achievement-Level Results, 2019

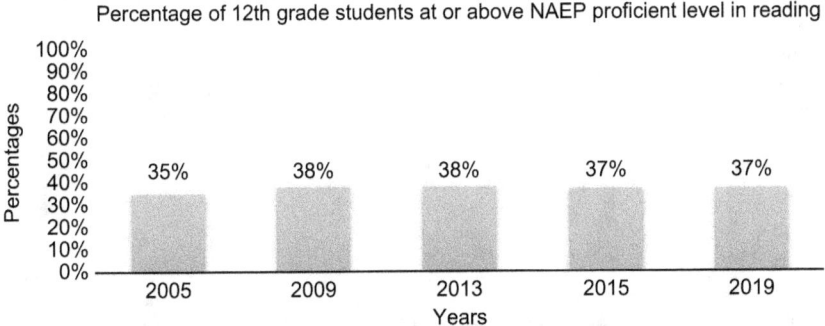

**FIGURE 3.2** Trends in twelfth-grade NAEP reading achievement-level results
Source: NAEP Readings: National Average Scores, 2019

**fewer than 7% of African American students in 12th grade are proficient or better in math, and 17% are proficient or better in reading.** This lack of attainment puts these students at risk of failure in college, technical training, or in the workplace (NAEP, 2015).

Indeed, it is clear that high school graduation does not ensure that you have the skills needed to be highly successful in the modern workplace. Over recent years this is something heard loudly from employers across the country, but also from the Joint Chiefs of Staff of the U.S. military. The days in which high school dropouts and kids in trouble with the law could

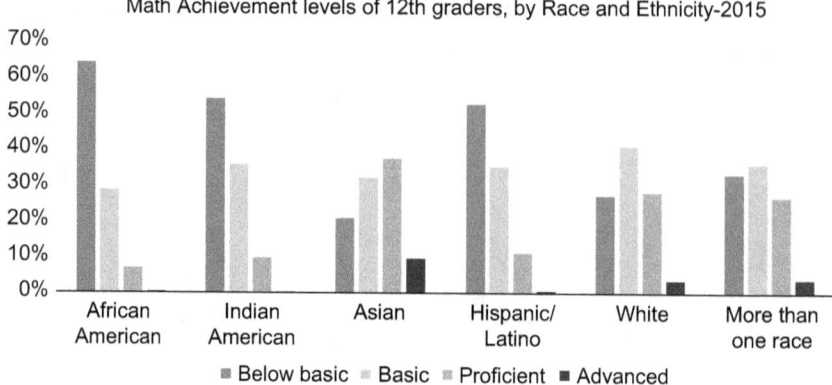

**FIGURE 3.3** Twelfth Grade Math Achievement Levels by Race and Ethnicity
Source: NAEP 12th-Grade Achievement Levels, 2015

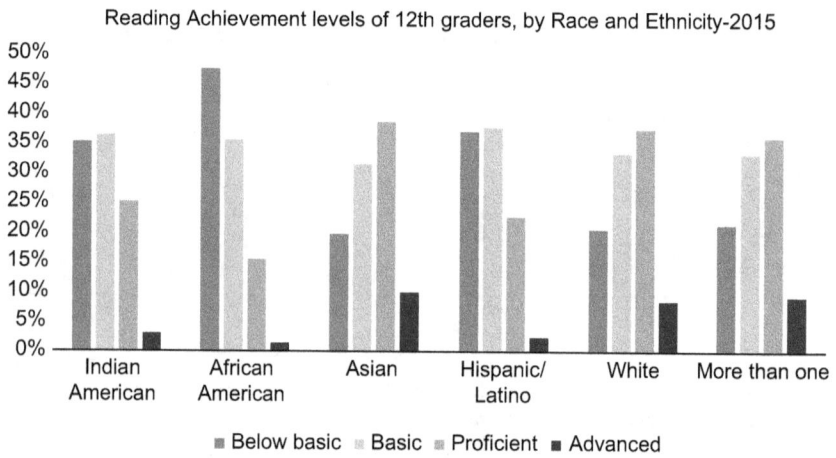

**FIGURE 3.4** Twelfth Grade Reading Achievement Levels by Race and Ethnicity
Source: NAEP 12 Grade Achievement Levels, 2015

easily join the military are long gone. Military service requires a capacity for learning, along with physical skills and character.

In 2009, a report prepared for the Joint Chiefs of Staff entitled *Ready, Willing and Unable to Serve,* concluded that about 75% of the country's 17- to 24-year-olds are ineligible for military service, largely because they are poorly educated, overweight, or have physical ailments that make them unfit for the armed forces. The Joint Chiefs have called this a national security issue.

More recent studies continue to see this same trend, reporting that about 71% of the country's 17- to 24-year-olds are ineligible for military service (Longley, 2021; Spoehr, 2018; Strong, 2019).

Rates of success in college further call into question the learning readiness of high school graduates. **Please note that this author does not support the idea of college for all.** There are technical and field-specific training programs that may be far better and less expensive for individual students than a typical college experience. But among those who choose college, the likelihood of completion certainly matters.

Among full-time first-time students who began seeking a bachelor's degree at a four-year institution in fall 2013, 63% completed the degree at that institution within six years (National Center for Education Statistics, 2019). But college completion does not necessarily guarantee a good job or future, since 41% of college graduates cannot find full-time work in their chosen profession (Redden, 2020).

So not all students finish high school (85%), and among high school graduates only 24% are proficient in math and 37% are proficient in reading. Upon graduation only 29% have the skills needed to enter the military. Among high school graduates, about 65% go to college each year, but only 63% of these students complete their degree within six years. And among those who complete their degree, about 59% find work in their chosen field.

Our international rankings further complete the picture that our learning outcomes are discouraging. Program for International Student Assessment (PISA) results continue to deliver the bad news that **American schools are not improving learning outcomes,** and compared to other advanced nations we are quickly falling behind.

| U.S. scores on PISA, 15-years-olds (2000-2015) | | | | | | |
|---|---|---|---|---|---|---|
| | 2000 | 2003 | 2006 | 2009 | 2012 | 2015 |
| Reading | 504 | 495 | | 500 | 498 | 497 |
| Math | | 483 | 474 | 487 | 481 | 470 |
| Science | | | 489 | 502 | 497 | 496 |

**FIGURE 3.5** Trends in U.S. Students PISA Scores
Source: PISA 2015 Results (Volume 1) Excellence and Equity in Education, Table 1.4a (Reading); Table 1.2.4a; Table 1.5.4a (Math)

Since the Program for International Student Assessment began in 2000, U.S. student outcomes have failed to show improvement. This lack of improvement contrasts with the results from many other nations, putting the U.S. at the disadvantage of producing students who rank poorly among students from competing economies. Compared with the OECD nations who participate in PISA, U.S. 15-year-old students rank 23rd out of 70 in Reading, 39th out of 70 in Math, and 25th out of 70 in Science.

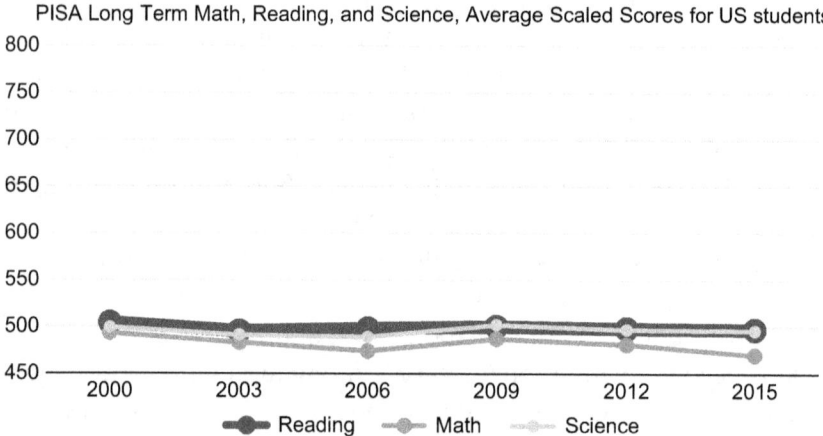

**FIGURE 3.6** Trends in U.S. Students PISA Scores Bar Chart
Source: Program for International Student Assessment (PISA) – Trends in Student Performance, 2015; Serino, L. (2017, April 7). What international test scores reveal about American education

**As an underlying cause for all poor learning outcomes,** this author has focused for many years on the need for a better system for educating young children. While there is a broad understanding that learning success during the PK to Grade 3 years predicts the trajectory of learning for life, there has been no significant shift in how we teach young children, except to add more content and pressure to the learning process. Early learning success is in part a parent responsibility, but from a systems perspective we must also look at building a system for learning in our schools that gives far more students the stable foundation needed to become great learners.

Young kids are not all the same. They develop at different rates and in different ways. Vygotsky, Piaget, Erikson, Gesell, Bowlby, Montessori, Gardner, Maslow, and other theorists help us understand and appreciate these differences. Everyone who has ever worked with young children can attest to the developmental variance and different learning needs of young children.

**And then these diverse children come to the typical school, a place in which all students are expected to be ready for grade-level content standards to be covered and tested in a time-limited learning system.** One-size-fits-all instruction and assessment quickly sorts kids into winners and losers. By the end of third grade, the last of the early childhood years, children have settled into patterns of learning that usually persist for life. And our system keeps creating far too many unsuccessful learners.

Since the early 1970s, the National Assessment of Educational Progress has monitored student-learning outcomes in each state and across the nation. After all the political shouting, after all the school reform initiatives, after all the billions of dollars spent on school reform, NAEP longitudinal data shows consistently poor early learning outcomes over time.

**By the beginning of fourth grade only 34% of American children are at proficient reading levels,** which predicts learning struggles for those non-proficient readers who will go onto the next years curriculum and content expectations whether they are fully prepared or not.

| Location | Achievement Level | Data type | 2002 | 2003 | 2005 | 2007 | 2009 | 2011 | 2013 | 2015 | 2017 | 2019 |
|---|---|---|---|---|---|---|---|---|---|---|---|---|
| United States | Below basic | Percent | 38% | 38% | 38% | 34% | 34% | 34% | 33% | 32% | 33% | 35% |
|  | At or above basic | Percent | 62% | 62% | 62% | 66% | 66% | 66% | 67% | 68% | 67% | 65% |
|  | Below proficient | Percent | 70% | 70% | 70% | 68% | 68% | 68% | 66% | 65% | 65% | 66% |
|  | At or above proficient | Percent | 30% | 30% | 30% | 32% | 32% | 32% | 34% | 35% | 35% | 34% |

**FIGURE 3.7** Trends in 4th Grade Reading Achievement in the U.S.
Source: Fourth Grade Reading Achievement Levels | KIDS COUNT Data Center, 2019; The Annie E. Casey Foundation, 2019

**These lousy reading results** are the same consistent outcomes that our curriculum-driven system for learning has produced for many years.

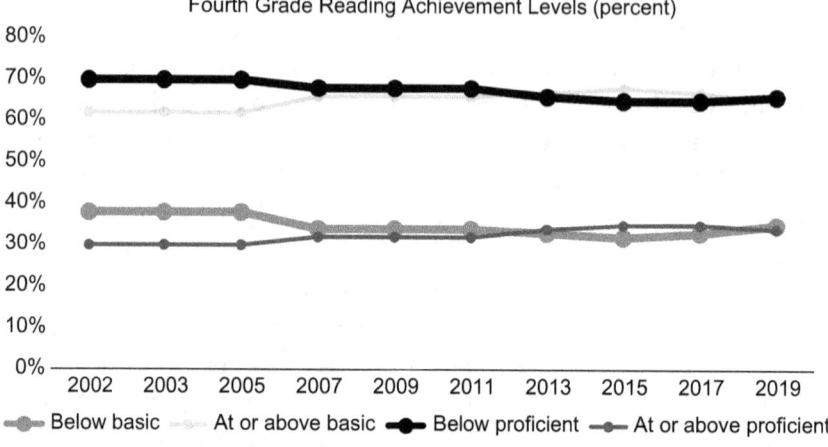

**FIGURE 3.8** Trends in 4th Grade Reading Achievement in the U.S. (Graphic)
Source: Fourth Grade Reading Achievement Levels | KIDS COUNT Data Center, 2019; The Annie E. Casey Foundation, 2019

**For poor children, the reading results are even worse.** Only 21% of fourth grade children who are eligible for free or reduced lunch are at proficient reading levels. That predicts that four out of five poor children are likely to be frustrated when participating in grade-level reading assignments from fourth grade until they finish school.

**In math, 4th grade achievement levels are also problematic.** Only 40% of all 4th grade students are proficient or better in mathematics (Annie E. Casey Foundation, 2019). This also reflects the long-term trend showing no discernible improvements in mathematics learning over recent decades.

**These lousy fourth grade math results** are the much like the outcomes that our curriculum-driven system for learning has produced for decades. If only 40% of students are proficient at 4th grade, then as the curriculum continues to be delivered at grade level for all students, we can predict that at least 60% of students will struggle in math learning.

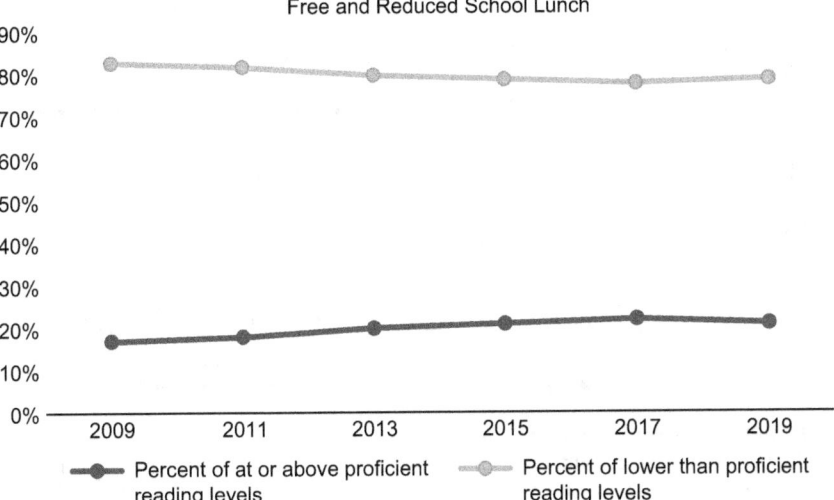

**FIGURE 3.9** Trends in 4th Grade Reading Achievement in the U.S. for Students Eligible for Free and Reduced School Lunch
Source: Fourth Grade Reading Achievement Levels | KIDS COUNT Data Center; The Annie E. Casey Foundation, 2019

| Location | Achievement Level | Data type | 2000 | 2003 | 2005 | 2007 | 2009 | 2011 | 2013 | 2015 | 2017 | 2019 |
|---|---|---|---|---|---|---|---|---|---|---|---|---|
| United States | Below basic | Percent | 36% | 24% | 21% | 19% | 19% | 18% | 18% | 19% | 21% | 20% |
| | At or above basic | Percent | 64% | 76% | 79% | 81% | 81% | 82% | 82% | 81% | 79% | 80% |
| | Below proficient | Percent | 78% | 69% | 65% | 61% | 62% | 60% | 59% | 61% | 60% | 60% |
| | At or above proficient | Percent | 22% | 31% | 35% | 39% | 38% | 40% | 41% | 39% | 40% | 40% |

**FIGURE 3.10** Trends in 4th grade mathematics
Source: Fourth Grade Mathematics Achievement Levels | KIDS COUNT Data Center; The Annie E. Casey Foundation, 2019

And by now you can also predict that **math outcomes for minority children** are particularly problematic. In the category of *better but not good enough* is the data on African American 4th grade math students. This group of students has seen a small improvement in scores over the last decades. 20% of black students were proficient or better on the fourth grade NAEP in 2019, up from 10% in 2003. But this small improvement is not

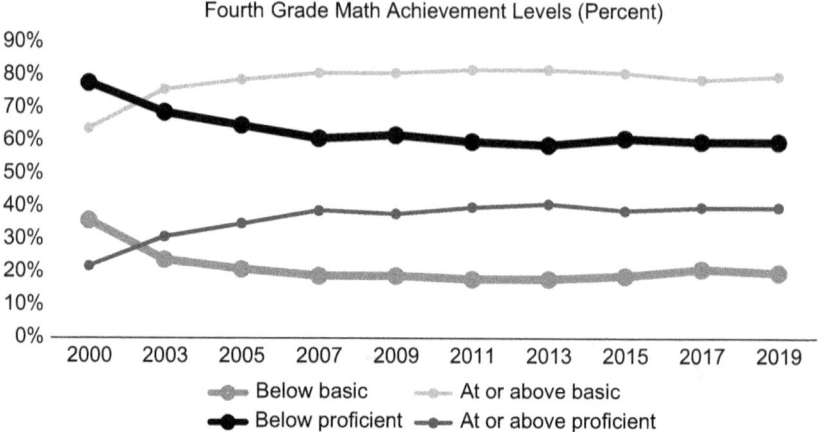

**FIGURE 3.11** Trends in 4th grade mathematics (Line Chart)
Source: Fourth Grade Mathematics Achievement Levels | KIDS COUNT Data Center, 2019; The Annie E. Casey Foundation, 2019

close to enough to help most African American high school grads be prepared for better jobs.

This 20% math proficiency figure significantly limits the likelihood of continued success in math learning to the 80% of black 4th grade students who are not proficient, **and directly impacts the unacceptably low 7% math proficiency outcome observed for African American 12th graders.**

**From a very practical societal perspective, our nation's inability to produce enough young men and women who are trained and ready for high skill and high pay jobs** should be forcing us to reconsider the model for learning that we have relied upon for so long. In recent years job openings have exceeded job seekers. We cannot find enough qualified workers for the jobs available.

In 2021, while 8.4 million Americans were looking for work, 10 million jobs continue to go unfilled due to the lack of match between skill requirements and the available workforce (Long et al., 2021).

Lacking the training needed for higher skill and higher pay jobs, many Americans cannot find a good job at the same time as many companies cannot find the right employees. It has become abundantly clear that our education system is not

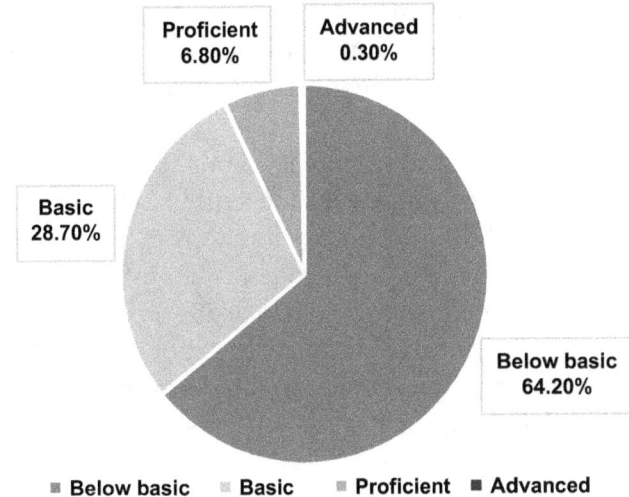

**FIGURE 3.12** 12th grade African American mathematics proficiency
Source: NAEP 12th-Grade Achievement Levels, 2015

**FIGURE 3.13** Trends in African American 4th grade students in Mathematics
Source: National Center for Education Statistics-Digest of Education Statistics, 2020

keeping up with the demand for qualified workers in an economy rich with opportunity for those who have the right skills and a capacity to learn.

**The Cover Test Sort model of education,** based on a system developed over a hundred years ago by Horace Mann and Frederick Winslow Taylor, is designed to cover content, test student learning, give grades, and then move forward to the next unit or lessons that are part of the curriculum. It was never designed to nurture competency in a majority of students, or to help large numbers of kids fall in love with learning for life. It was never designed for the age of ideas, technology, and innovation.

Our world has certainly changed in the last 50 years, but not our system for providing education within schools. More kids are staying in school, and graduating from high school, but a majority graduate without grade-level proficiency in math, reading, and science. Many of the skills needed for success on the job are not priorities within our schools, including social skills based on empathy, resilience, problem-solving, collaboration, technical skills, and entrepreneurial skills.

> **What would you want for your own children?**
>
> **This question serves as a guide for decision makers. Does our existing system adequately prepare a majority of students for the realities of life in the mid-21st century?**

Lacking a model in which essential learning outcomes are identified and then carefully developed using personalized competency based learning, we have continued to pursue content coverage and testing with vigor. Here are some of the results:

- By the beginning of fourth grade only 34% of American children are at proficient reading levels (National Assessment of Educational Progress, 2019).
- Only 21% of fourth grade children who are eligible for free or reduced lunch are at proficient reading levels (National Assessment of Educational Progress, 2019).
- Only 20% of fourth grade African American children are at proficient levels in math (National Assessment of Educational Progress, 2019).
- Among 12th grade students (remember that a significant group of students has already dropped out by this point),

24% of students score at or above proficient levels in math, and 37% are proficient or better in reading (National Assessment of Educational Progress, 2019).
- Among African American twelfth grade students tested, 7% are proficient or better in math and 17% are proficient or better in reading (National Assessment of Educational Progress, 2019).
- The Joint Chiefs of Staff report that about 71% of the country's 17- to 24-year-olds are ineligible for military service (Mission Readiness, 2009; Longley, 2021; Spoehr, 2018; Strong, 2019).
- 63% of full-time first-time students who began seeking a bachelor's degree at a four-year institution in fall 2013 completed the degree at that institution within six years (NCES 2019).
- 41% of college graduates cannot find full-time work in their chosen profession (Redden, 2020).
- With 8.4 million Americans looking for work and millions more settling for part-time jobs, 10 million plus jobs continue to go unfilled due to the lack of match between skill requirements and the available workforce (Long et al., 2021).

**Using our existing Cover Test Sort model, we continue to produce astonishing numbers of non-proficient K-12 students, high school dropouts, dropouts from institutions of advanced learning, and college grads without the skills to compete in the workplace. How could it be any different?**

# 4
# Without Learning Competency There Can Be No Equity

> The American Dream – the idea that anyone who is determined and works hard can get ahead – has long defined the promise of the United States. Yet the reality is that life chances for Americans are now determined to a significant degree by the wealth of our parents. The dream that hard work and playing by the rules will lead to greater opportunity and a steady climb up the economic ladder is increasingly challenging to achieve, particularly for struggling families.
> – Annie E. Casey Foundation (2014)

Hard work still counts, **but hard physical work without competency in academic, social-emotional, and technical skills is unlikely to be enough** to allow young men and women to find success in the information and technology economy. Auto factories which once employed thousands of men and women, now operate with a staff of hundreds, each with technical skills and responsibilities. Farmers, tool and die makers, service providers, and manufacturers increasingly rely on equipment that requires reading and computing, and on employees who can regularly learn to use new systems and procedures.

While millions of low skill workers compete for low-wage jobs, more than ten million jobs which require high skill workers go unfilled in the American economy.

### A World of Opportunity

If you happen to be proficient in reading and math, with a deep love of learning, intrinsically motivated to learn for life, with strong social-emotional skills, self-regulation skills, collaboration skills, problem-solving skills, and character, this is a world filled with opportunities.

With our continued reliance on the CTS model, only a small segment of our society becomes proficient in reading and math, develops a deep love of learning, becomes intrinsically motivated to learn throughout life, has strong social-emotional skills, and has the self-regulation and character skills to focus and persevere. For those who have these skill sets, living in the information age is rich with opportunity. Businesses and organizations are looking hard for these young men and women.

**The world of opportunity has never been fair.** There have always been advantages that some people have based on birth, gender, wealth, connections, or opportunities to learn which other people did not have. But in the age of ideas and innovation, the divide between rich and poor is growing.

In spite of this lack of equality of opportunity, a child's capacity to think and learn, work collaboratively and solve complex problems, will greatly contribute to the pattern of opportunities they will encounter in their lives. Education has long been considered a pathway to opportunity. But at present we use a broken system that fails to give most disadvantaged kids the skills and knowledge they need to compete.

From a global perspective, the richest 10% of the global population currently earn 52% of annual income, while the poorest half of the global population earn just 8%. The wealth gap is even greater. Wealth includes valuable assets and items (above income). The poorest half of the global population owns just 2% of global assets, while the richest 10% own 76% of all wealth (World Inequality Report, 2022).

In the United States, the top 1% now own more wealth than the bottom 92%, and the 50 wealthiest Americans own more wealth than the 165 million people in the bottom half of the wealth distribution. While millions of Americans have lost their jobs and incomes during the pandemic, many billionaires have seen their wealth increase. The middle class is shrinking, leaving a small wealthy class and a much larger under-class. Now, and in the foreseeable future, it will take real skills to work your way from poverty to a more rewarding life.

This book does not address tax and economic policy, for lots of good reasons (including my lack of expertise). It does address the role our schools play in creating opportunities for children as they learn and grow. Poverty matters in this discussion. **Child poverty is associated with reduced skill-building opportunities and academic outcomes,** undercutting a young student's capacity to learn, graduate high school, and get high-skill high-wage jobs.

Simply put for the purposes of this book, children living with many of the disadvantages associated with poverty need schools that respond to their specific learning needs and offer a system of learning to help them become competent learners. **Vulnerable kids need better schools,** based on a much different model of education than the Cover Test Sort model that has been producing the same lousy outcomes for decades.

Keep in mind that the damage caused by our one-size-fits all education system is not limited to those students living in poverty. Indeed, **a majority of all students are not proficient readers and mathematicians in 4th grade, 8th grade, and 12th grade.** The calamity of becoming a struggling learner is crushing poor kids, but also crushing a majority of all our children.

Let's examine some data points from the previous chapter. Among 12th grade students (remember that a significant group of students has already dropped out by this point), 24% of students score at or above proficient levels in math, and 37% are proficient or better in reading (National Assessment of Educational Progress, 2019).

**If approximately one-third of graduating high school students are reading proficiently, then two-thirds are not!** Reading well is a factor in being successful in college, in the military, or in a trade. Reading is a factor in finding a job, becoming a successful entrepreneur, and will be a factor in being employable in the future. But our CTS system of learning is consistently failing to help a large majority of kids develop proficiency in reading.

**If approximately one-quarter of graduating high school students are doing math proficiently, then three-quarters are not!** Math matters. Poor math skills limit a person's interaction with the world of technology, learning, and innovation. Math is a factor in finding a job, becoming a successful entrepreneur, and will be a factor in staying employable in the future. But the CTS system of learning is consistently failing to help a large majority of kids develop mathematics proficiency.

Here is another data point that should be shocking, appalling, and unacceptable. **Among African American twelfth grade students tested, 7% are proficient or better in math and 17% are proficient or better in reading (National Assessment of Educational Progress, 2019).** Does anyone find this acceptable? If it is not acceptable, then how many of you readers have spoken up loudly, demanding a system redesign that produces better results?

> **How can anyone working for racial equity believe that we can achieve equitable outcomes for African American students in our society without fixing a system that has consistently allowed so many black American kids to become struggling learners for life?**

By relying as we do on the Cover Test Sort methodology of our curriculum-driven schools, the effects of poverty on school success and life success will continue to haunt generations of students. Unless schools and parents step up to the responsibility to help far more of our children develop competency in the skills that could allow them to become successful learners, millions of poor or vulnerable students will fail to develop the skills that lead to a decent job and a productive life. Unless we redesign our schools, poverty will increasingly beget learning failure and more poverty. Without skills that matter to employers, most poor children are doomed to economic and social hardship. Without rock-solid learning skills and social skills, a vast majority of poor children face will continue to face poverty for life.

> **There was a time when determination and hard work, without having well developed reading and math skills, could lead to success. That day is long gone. A new day has arrived, in which learning success must be part of the formula for life success. Becoming a successful learner is a necessary part of the path toward the American dream.**

# 5

# Giving Up Unproductive Mental Models

So much of what we do in schools is based on continuing familiar patterns of belief and behavior. Here are a few mental models **whose time is up.**

## UMM #1. Academic Rigor is Demonstrated by Covering More Content in Each Grade

In 1983, the President's Commission on Excellence in Education published its report, *A Nation at Risk: The Imperative for Educational Reform.* The report famously stated, **"The educational foundations of our society are presently being eroded by a rising tide of mediocrity that threatens our very future as a Nation and a people. If an unfriendly foreign power had attempted to impose on America the mediocre educational performance that exists today, we might well have viewed it as an act of war."** The report supported the idea that American schools were failing, and touched off a wave of state and federal reform efforts which continue to this day. The 1989 Bush Education Summit, Goals 2000, NCLB, Race to the Top, and ESEA waivers are rooted in the same political soil, based on the belief that legislative action and Department of Education regulations could improve education outcomes.

Under pressure to improve performance, the curriculum-driven assembly line model responded by doing more of what a curriculum-driven assembly line model does. **We added more content expectations. We asked teachers to cover content more quickly. We added more testing to ensure that all the content was being covered. We added pacing guides and district pacing assessments. Many schools adopted scripted one-size-fits-all reading and math programs to ensure that everything was being covered. We began to grade and fail schools. We began to require evaluation of teachers based on student learning outcomes on standardized state assessments.**

Teachers have felt the pressure to "cover" for several decades. In a comparison of U.S. curricula to that of high achieving countries (Schmidt et al, 2001, 2005, 2009), the number of science and math topics covered in U.S. school is significantly greater, and the amount of repetition of content from grade to grade is almost double that of the better achieving school systems.

Schmoker and Marzano (1999) advised educators, "We will realize the promise of school reform when we establish standards and expectations for reaching them that are clear, not confusing; essential, not exhaustive. The result will be a new coherence and a shared focus that could be the most propitious step we can take toward educating all students well."

Viable content is the content that can be reasonably covered in the time available. In *What Works in Schools* (2003), Robert Marzano ranks a guaranteed and viable content as the factor having the most impact on student achievement.

> **The National Council of Teachers of Mathematics recommends that math curriculum should include fewer topics, spending enough time to make sure each is learned in enough depth that it need not be revisited in later grades. That is the approach used in most top-performing nations.**
> – National Mathematics Advisory Council, 2008

> **If you wanted to cover all of the standards in the national documents, you would have to change schooling from K-12 to K-22.**
>
> - 255 standards across 14 subject areas
> - 3,500 benchmarks
> - 13,000 hours of class time available
> - 9,000 hours of instruction available
> - 15,500 hours of instruction needed to cover the 3,500 benchmarks
>
> – Robert Marzano (2006)

In spite of consistent recommendations to slow down the pace of instruction, there is little evidence that anyone is listening. In recent years, the narrative to the Common Core State Standards calls over and over to us to cover fewer topics to a deeper level of understanding so that topics do not need to be retaught in subsequent grades. But the fear of not being ready for the mandated state and national tests seems to have limited our ability to respond thoughtfully and truly narrow the scope of instructional content.

According to *The Reality of College Readiness* (ACT, 2021), only 25% of the 1.8 million students taking the ACT exam are college-ready in math, reading, English, and science. ACT has defined "college and career readiness" as the acquisition of knowledge and skills a student needs to enroll and succeed in credit-bearing first-year college courses at a postsecondary institution without the need for remediation.

In 2013, slightly more than one-fourth of ACT-tested graduates did not meet any of the four college readiness benchmarks. By 2021 the percentage of students **meeting none of the four benchmarks** increased to 38%.

> **In a report by the Educational Testing Service, *America's Skills Challenge: Millennials and the Future* (2015), the ETS compared literacy, numeracy, and problem solving**

> skills of 16 to 34 year olds in 22 countries using data from the OECD Programme for International Assessment of Adult Competencies. In literacy, US millennials scored lower than 15 other nations. In both numeracy and problem solving, US millennials were tied for last.

*Ready, Willing and Unable to Serve* (Mission Readiness, 2009), a report prepared for the Joint Chiefs of Staff, concluded that about 75% of the country's 17- to 24-year-olds are ineligible for military service, largely because they are poorly educated, overweight, or have physical ailments that make them unfit for the armed forces. Updates to this document have adjusted that estimate to 71% ineligible. The Joint Chiefs have called this a national security issue. Those days when the armed services welcomed young men and women with behavior and learning problems are long gone.

ETS's Irwin Kirsch, in the preface to *America's Skills Challenge*, stated: "This report suggests that far too many are graduating high school and completing postsecondary educational programs without receiving adequate skills. If we expect to have a better educated population and a more competitive workforce, policy makers and other stakeholders will need to shift the conversation from one of educational attainment to one that acknowledges the growing importance of skills and examines these more critically." (ETS, 2015)

The proof is in the pudding. By now, the dismal results that our coverage based one-size-fits-all model produce should be clear to any observer. Cover Test Sort does not meet the needs of a vast majority of students.

When it comes to human learning, quantity of coverage does not equate to quality. Our curriculum-driven instructional model, on steroids since the advent of national school reform initiatives, has consistently failed to help more students love learning, or to attain high levels of skill in literacy, numeracy, science, or problem-solving. The poor are especially vulnerable to the adverse effects of this model, but all of students suffer from our continued reliance on this design for teaching and learning.

Racing through large volumes of content does not lead to better learning outcomes. Give it up!

## UMM #2. Grading on the Bell Curve

In probability theory, normal (or Gaussian) distribution is typically described by use of a bell curve, which shows the mean and standard variation from the mean. One deviation from the mean is comprised of approximately one-third of the total, and everything within one standard deviation up and one standard deviation down is statistically normal.

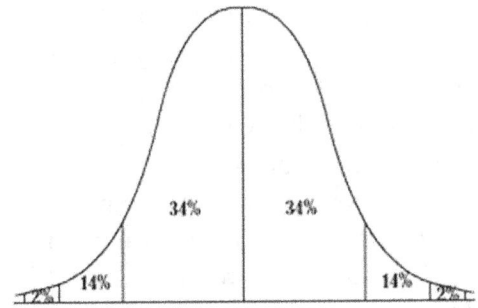

**FIGURE 5.1** A bell curve

The bell curve is an important statistical tool used to analyze large sets of data and to determine what is typical, and to predict probable outcomes. In education, the use of the bell curve was adopted to determine normal distribution and assign grades based on a comparison with other students.

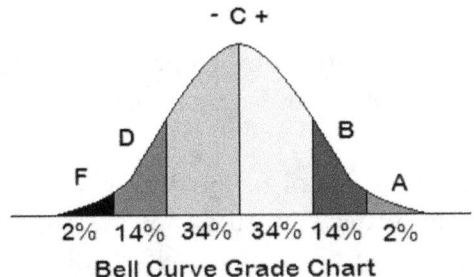

**FIGURE 5.2** Bell Curve Grade Chart

When used for grading, a bell curve ensures a balanced distribution of grades, with only a small percentage receiving the highest or the lowest grades. Over the years, mostly in response to pressure from parents, the grading "curve" has shifted to include far more B's and A's than the standard distribution.

The Gaussian Distribution is the statistical foundation for all of our state and national standardized testing. Numeric scores on standardized assessments are converted to percentiles. At the 50th percentile, half the scores are better and half the scores are worse. At the 90th percentile, your score is better than 90% of the other scores. At the 10th percentile, your score is better than 10% of the other scores.

Use of a bell curve for grading can be misleading. As an example, imagine two high school English Language Arts instructors. One is an experienced and highly professional teacher who diligently pursues high level reading and writing skills for her students. The other teacher has been waiting for retirement for the past decade, does no class preparation, and often reads the newspaper in class. Both classes are receiving instruction in English, but the quality of instruction and learning varies significantly. In both classes there is a normal distribution of grades, based on a loosely applied bell curve model.

In the more professional teacher's classroom, eight students earned an A grade. In the less professional teacher's classroom, eight students earned an A grade. But a careful analysis of reading and writing skills shows that B-grade students in the professional teacher's class have far better writing skills than A-grade students in the slacker teacher's classroom.

**Coverage does not infer competency, and typical grading structures do not measure competency.**

The Bell Curve is a tool for analyzing normal distribution among large sets of data, but it is not designed to tell which students are competent in any specific skill. In James' third grade math class, his teacher managed to "cover" every CCSS math standard. Using a math program in which all children get the same instruction on the same day in exactly the same way, the instructional plan directed the teacher to "cover" every content standard. There was no identification of essential math skills or concepts, and therefore no systematic measurement of progress toward these crucial outcomes. From week to week the teacher delivered lessons without going back to offer needy students more time or instruction to understand important skills at a deeper level.

Grades were awarded based on a bell curve model, identifying some as A math students, and some as D math students. A few of the students had a very poor understanding of important math concepts but were great at memorizing facts and formulas. They scored well on tests.

These math memorizers received A's or B's. But their lack of deep understanding of important skills and concepts will likely cause them difficulty when they reach higher levels of math, for which memory of facts will not suffice.

At the end of the third grade, each child was given a D, C, B, or A in math. James was identified as a B-level student in math. Not bad, he thought, compared with some of the other kids, not realizing that he had not yet fully developed key math skills even close to competency. Not realizing that math learning in the future would soon become difficult and frustrating. Not realizing that compromised development of crucial math skills would limit his working options for the rest of his life.

Use of the Bell Curve is an anachronism that fits nicely with the cover and sort model, but does not help demonstrate whether students have achieved competency in understanding content or developing skills. Give it up!

## UMM #3. Creating Winners and Losers

There are times when rigorous coverage is a useful tool for sorting out which students should be allowed to continue in a program, and which should not. Astronaut training puts candidates through a difficult course of training to decide which candidates have the right stuff. The first phases of training for medical doctors are purposefully difficult, and serve to sort some students out of the process.

Navy Seals and Army Rangers go through an incredibly demanding series of training activities; and the vast majority of candidates do not make it. But the ones who do make it are the best candidates for these dangerous and demanding jobs.

When the program or profession only needs a small number of new members, and many people would like to be among this group, rigorous coverage and training are one way to help sort out the candidates who are diligent, ready to learn, and resilient.

King of the Raft is played with the goal of finding one winner among a group of other non-winners. Dodge ball is based on the same principle. Who is quickest, strongest, and has the best aim?

**Curriculum-driven instructional fits nicely with the King of the Raft philosophy of schools. Teach fast and hard and see which kids survive.**

Good students and bad students. Red birds and black birds. Honor society and all the rest. Our system has consistently created a small pool of good readers and a whole lot of kids who hate to read. CTS programming creates a small number of math superstars and a vast majority of students who avoid math throughout their lives and careers.

We continue to use systems that identify students who are "good" at instruction that was presented at one moment in time. We create winners and losers rather than recognizing that children have differing learning experiences and learning rates, and that from any starting point students can build high-quality learning skills that matter.

In 1910, when fewer than 10% of students graduated from high school, the curriculum-driven one-size-fits-all model worked well-enough. In the modern world, schools based on this model are harming many children. Educators communicate the expectations of our curriculum driven model in a variety of ways.

- *I have to keep up with the pacing guide.*
- *I am expected to cover all the chapters.*
- *I can't wait around for just a few kids who don't get it.*
- *Spiraling. Someday we will revisit this concept that so many kids don't understand*
- *We have to get ready for the test.*
- *The government requires that we cover all this material.*
- *You are expected to already know how to do this.*
- *If you'd only concentrate.*
- *If you'd do your homework.*
- *If you'd come to school on time.*
- *If you didn't miss so many days.*
- *Today I am covering CCSS.MATH.CONTENT.6.RP.A.3.*

There are so many ways to say it. *I am teaching the content and you are expected to keep up. If you don't keep up, and more than two-thirds of you won't, it's on you. If you get sick and miss some days, or are the youngest in your class, or live in a chaotic home, or learn differently, or carry the burden of high levels of stress, you will probably get left behind.*

The process of creating (or discerning) Winners and Losers is a horribly destructive anachronism. Give it up!

**For decades American schools have been engaged in a failed experiment,** attempting to cram more content into a typical teaching day than humanly possible, asking children to learn overwhelming content at younger and younger ages, and not taking the time to help every child build the foundation skills needed for lifelong learning success. We race through instruction in the same way for all kids, give grades that judge you rather than help you identify the specific skills and concepts you need to learn, and create educational winners and losers, mostly losers.

Sixty years ago the United States had the best educated workforce in the world. Since then we've created anxiety-filled classrooms in which children are less likely to fall deeply in love with learning, and where thoughtful teachers struggle to love their work. We continued to use a more is better, test it harder system which compares outcomes but does not support the development of competency. We've created a system that aggressively identifies the winners from the losers, but has not made any progress toward reducing the number of losers.

**Building crucial learning skills is not a race.** By carefully identifying and then slowing down the pace of instruction for essential skills, and by allowing every child to fully develop these skills we could improve the learning future of our children. As we evolve from a curriculum driven educational design to a competency based learning model we will establish a different framework that clearly identifies crucial learning outcomes, considers the learning steps along a pathway to important life skills, tracks student progress toward crucial outcomes, personalizes instruction, and supports teachers as they offer instruction that meets the needs of each student.

# 6

# Building a New Model

A competency based learning system **begins with the premise that we truly want each student to succeed.** Rather than letting the pacing guide dictate the delivery of instruction, students learning dictates how we plan instruction. Individual students move ahead toward higher-level learning outcomes by demonstrating that they fully understand key learning skills along the path to higher level skills. Students will have as many learning opportunities as they need to develop these crucial skills, and each student is guaranteed to have the support needed to continue learning at their own pace as they progress toward crucial outcomes.

This learner-centered model is a significant departure from the **more is better, test it harder, winners and losers system** we have created in most of our schools. With a better understanding of how kids learn, and with the information and technology systems that are now available, we can choose to track progress toward crucial outcomes and develop thoughtful pathways to mastery of the skills needed for learning, life and workplace success.

Much of this is just the application of common sense. In the non-school parts of our lives, whenever a learning goal has been identified as "crucial" we try hard to develop personalized competency based learning experiences for our children. When teaching a young child to throw and catch, we refuse to follow a pacing guide. Instead we take the time to play, ensure high rates of success, and gradually increase challenge without causing frustration and disengagement.

When teaching a teenager to drive a car, wise parents take all the necessary time to practice driving in the school parking lot before moving to the side roads, and all the time needed on the side roads before moving to the main roads, and all the time needed on main roads before moving to the expressways, and all the time needed driving during good weather conditions until allowing your child to drive in more difficult weather.

> **No rational adult would throw a small hard ball at a child who is not fully able to catch it. Why then does math instruction in most schools consistently throw hardballs at kids who aren't ready?**

Math instruction is among the conspicuous failures of U.S. schools. It is a classic example of too much content, delivered too fast using a rigid pacing process, and advancing students to higher levels of learning without the deep understanding of fundamental concepts and skills needed for long-term success. Consider these kindergarten math skills that are crucial for understanding higher level math concepts:

- Has one-to-one correspondence for numbers 1–30.
- Understands combinations to 10.
- Recognizes number groups (2 to 10) without counting.

> **One-to-one correspondence is the ability to count concrete objects or movements with accuracy. Some children can say the numerals in sequence, but do not yet have the connection to associate "three" with 3 button, "four" with 4 buttons, etc. Lacking one-to- one correspondence children might say a number without really understanding its value.**

> Understanding combinations to 10 includes the ability to use one-to-one correspondence to show you "four buttons", then add "two buttons" and quickly figure out that now there are six buttons". Using real objects or movements they can demonstrate any combination of numbers adding up to 10 or less.
>
> Recognizing number groups (2 to 10) without counting is the ability to look at a domino, or a die, or any pattern of dots, beads, chairs, etc. and quickly name the value. This skill is sometimes called "subitizing", and assumes some understanding of both one-to-one.

In a personalized learning kindergarten environment, children would be carefully monitored for the development of these crucial math skills. Instruction would be matched to the child's readiness, so that some children might practice counting objects, while other children are working combinations. Some children would likely develop every one of these skills by January, while others would need hands-on and movement based activities for these skills until April or May. Only when a child can perform a skill easily, with a high rate of success, using a variety of learning materials, would they be considered competent.

Each child would be given as much time as needed and as much differentiated learning practice as needed for these essential learning outcomes, until competency is well established. But classroom instruction might also include lessons that "introduce, cover, or explore" additional content including measurement, estimation, equations, sets, and many other topics that can be enjoyed in small groups, centers, or whole group settings. Instruction becomes a blend of exploration activities that build a general understanding of math, along with carefully designed and differentiated instruction aimed toward competency in the specifically designated essential learning outcomes.

**In a curriculum-driven kindergarten learning environment,** all children would be given the same lesson on the same day in the same way. Early in the year, maybe even from the first day, math instruction would be delivered using worksheets, without access to the touching, moving, feeling experiences which are integral to understanding these basic skills. Students would be encouraged to memorize facts they do not understand, or follow a series of steps to get an answer they can only hope might be right. Many of these students would move on to higher grades lacking number sense, not really understanding combination or number values.

If math learning outcomes are important to a child's future **(and they are)**, some skills deserve all the time, instruction, and attention needed to help every child develop competency. Throwing math hardballs at young children creates frustrated math phobic students who will disengage from math learning for life. American millennials, tied for last place among the 22 countries evaluated in the OECD Programme for International Assessment of Adult Competencies (ETS, 2015) in math and problem solving, give evidence of the poor outcomes associated with curriculum-driven math instruction.

Competency based learning challenges many of the traditional practices of our schools:

- CBL suggests that instruction be designed to respond to specific student learning needs and support student progress toward clearly defined learning outcomes.
- The competency model requires a capacity for differentiation, allowing students to learn in different ways, and giving all the time needed for the development of proficiency for crucial skills.
- CBL requires the articulation of a clear sequence of learning objectives which lead to the desired outcomes, and a plan for on-going assessment of progress.

**In the competency model, students are not passed along with significant gaps in understanding which cause them to fall further and further behind. For the identified crucial learning outcomes, instruction is designed to**

match the developmental readiness of the students, so that they are engaged and challenged but not frustrated. Students advance upon mastery to higher levels of skill and challenge.

Competency based learning approaches are typically designed around five key elements (CompetencyWorks, 2018):

1. Students advance upon mastery.
2. Competencies include explicit, measurable, transferable learning objectives that empower students.
3. Assessment is meaningful and a positive learning experience for students.
4. Students receive timely, differentiated support based on their individual learning needs.
5. Learning outcomes emphasize competencies that include application and creation of knowledge, along with the development of important skills and dispositions.

Personalized learning leading to competency is in evidence when a high-quality piano teacher carefully observes her student, challenges her to improve by giving her the assignment to learn a beautiful piece of music which is within her ability range, offers timely but not overwhelming suggestions for pacing and hand position, and gives her all the time needed to learn the music and be ready for a successful performance.

Learning is personalized when a computer tech student studies for a test, and comes up short, is given immediate feedback on the answers that were incorrect and the opportunity to study some more and take the test again as soon as he is ready.

Personalized learning is built into the structure of quality digital math and reading programs. A clearly defined sequence of skills leads to competency. Essential steps in the sequence cannot be hurried through or avoided. **At each step in the sequence of skills, competency must be demonstrated,** and only then a student moves forward to the next tier of instruction.

The Khan Academy is a well-designed example of this structure which is built with competency as the goal for each student.

A preschool to grade three competency based math system, *Essential Math Skills* (Sornson, 2014) identifies a competency framework for the early childhood years, including a small set of target math outcomes for each grade. Teachers are encouraged to offer a rich and interesting curriculum filled with activities and projects, while carefully monitoring progress toward this set of crucial outcomes. Some children may need to work on skills from the previous grade level. Others will be working at grade level, and still others will be working on skills from a more advanced level. **Proficiency for each crucial skill will only be noted when a student has demonstrated deep understanding, over a period of time, using a variety of learning materials to ensure both understanding and application.**

A personalized graduate school program identifies the crucial minimum skills for competency in your field of study, assesses student skill levels, with the help of a mentor designs plans for learning which can include courses, work experiences, independent learning experiences, on-line courses, apprenticeships and other experiences, and then carefully monitors progress toward competency. Some students progress faster than others. **Only when competency has been clearly demonstrated for each crucial outcome is the degree awarded.**

Personalized learning is in evidence on the job as employees work to attain new skills, are given both written and real life assessments, and develop a personal portfolio of skills that are valuable to the employer and offer opportunities for advancement.

**A competency structure values learning over seat time.** Accumulated Carnegie units or CEUs are not the coin of the realm in a competency based learning model. Rather, deep learning and the capacity to apply information and skills are the valued outcomes of competency based learning. A competency structure gives students the time they need to develop a crucial skill or concept. Six weeks may not be enough for some. Other students may be ready to move on more quickly. Lack of competency after the specified time for a course is not a life sentence. Within a competency model of instruction, critical skills are given the necessary time to develop.

**A competency based system is designed to help every student become proficient in clearly defined essential outcomes,** and lays out the steps leading to those outcomes. Instruction is designed so that students are in their optimal developmental zone as much as possible, so that they are challenged but not pushed into frustration and disengagement. In a competency based learning system students are not passed along from grade to grade with significant gaps in understanding, skill, and application.

> **In a proficiency system, failure or poor performance may be part of the student's learning curve, but it is not an outcome.**
> – Oregon Education Roundtable (2009)

Crucial learning outcomes warrant personalized competency based learning. When coverage, enrichment, exposure, or an overview are not enough, competency based learning provides the path to achieving these outcomes. We want our children to develop competency before getting a driver's license because basic driving skills are crucial to their survival. **Doctors, astronauts, electricians, and computer techs go through a competency based learning program to assure that every essential skill has been fully developed** so that they have the expertise needed for success.

Competency based learning works best when there are clearly defined learning objectives, a step-by-step plan for developing those skills, a careful assessment of the learner's skills and readiness, instruction at the student's developmental level, continued monitoring of progress, and instruction adjusted to her changing levels of skill until competency is achieved.

Every parent teaching their child to ride a bike knows how to design a personalized learning program leading to competency. It may take a year of practice before the training wheels come off. There may be a prolonged period in which you run alongside the bike to steady it as needed. There may even be a bump or bruise along the way, but with patience, your child learns to ride independently with confidence and skill.

# 7

# Principles of Instruction Leading to Competency

Principles of Instruction Leading to Competency

1. Identify a manageable set of crucial outcomes to be the focus of on-going assessment and instruction.
2. Assess the learning needs of your students to determine skill levels and readiness for instruction.
3. Develop an instructional plan (curriculum) that allows you to teach a rich and interesting course of study while regularly monitoring progress toward essential outcomes.
4. Deliver instruction to match the learning needs of your students. Move proficient students on to more challenging learning opportunities, give developing students time to fully develop essential outcomes, and offer intensive support to students who need it.
5. Monitor progress toward essential outcomes consistently throughout the instructional process, and adapt the level of difficulty so that students are challenged but never overwhelmed.

> 6. **Never compromise the standards of proficiency for an essential skill. These skills are crucial for success and deserve all the time needed for the development of competence.**

The implementation of competency based learning relies on our ability to build a new model for instruction and learning. In the decades to come, we will build upon principles which are substantially different than those of the Cover-Test-Sort curriculum-driven model. In this chapter, we consider six principles for instruction leading to competency.

1. **Identify a manageable set of crucial outcomes to be the focus of on-going assessment and instruction.**
   Begin with the end in mind. Identify crucial learning outcomes, and establish clear milestones for progress so it is possible to monitor progress toward annual and long-term learning goals. Rather than giving teachers the mandate to "cover" a set of overwhelming content expectations, competency based learning must establish clear learning outcomes so that every teacher and every student knows exactly what is expected and needed for success. These crucial outcomes must be both clear and concise, establishing a framework of skills and knowledge that can be assessed by giving students multiple means and opportunities to demonstrate mastery through performance-based and other assessments.
2. **Assess the learning needs of your students to determine skill levels and readiness for instruction.**
   Rather than asking, "What was covered in the previous grade?" the competency based teacher will assess what students know and what they are ready to learn. If content was covered, but not learned, developing deep understanding of more complex content will be difficult or impossible until fundamental skills are learned. If students already have deep understanding

of the prescribed grade level content, they are ready to advance to higher levels of learning.

3. **Develop an instructional plan (curriculum) that allows you to teach a rich and interesting course of study while regularly monitoring progress toward essential outcomes.**

   Competency based instruction will enhance a love of learning and introduce students to new ideas and ways to learn. A quality course of study includes activities, projects, and opportunities to extend and integrate learning. Schools may wish to use curriculum maps and/or pacing guides to create an overall framework for instruction in the school, but within that instructional framework there will be time and support for each student to develop crucial skills on the pathway to important academic and social-emotional outcomes.

4. **Deliver instruction to match the learning needs of your students. Move proficient students on to more challenging learning opportunities, give developing students time to fully develop essential outcomes, and offer intensive support to students who need it.**

   Some instruction can be delivered as an introduction, overview, or even "coverage" of content. But essential outcomes will be held to the highest standard. Students learn best when offered instruction or learning opportunities that are a little bit challenging but not so difficult as to cause consistent failure, frustration, or disengagement. Crucial instruction will be designed to fit the needs of students, and delivered in their instructional zone. This approach increases motivation to learn, time on task, and improves learning outcomes.

5. **Monitor progress toward essential outcomes consistently throughout the instructional process, and adapt the level of difficulty so that students are challenged but never overwhelmed.**

   As student skill levels improve, crucial instruction is adapted to meet the readiness levels of each student. Teachers carefully monitor progress through performance based, observational, and other assessments to know when to give students more time and when to accelerate learning.

6. **Never compromise the standards of proficiency for an essential skill. These skills are crucial for success and deserve all the time needed for the development of competence.**

   Competency is demonstrated by learning content or a skill so well that it would be difficult to unlearn, so that you can use it in everyday life, and apply it in multiple circumstances. Competency must be assessed cautiously, noting the student's skill or knowledge in multiple circumstances and multiple occasions.

**A competency based learning system is designed to enhance learning outcomes for our students, but also to give teachers a much better chance to succeed.** In recent decades, U.S. education has taken a public relations beating. No longer does the United States have the preeminent educational system in the world. No longer do we have the best educated workforce in the world.

Having worked in public education for many decades, it is my observation that teachers and principals are among the most caring and hardest working people around (with only a few exceptions). As long as we hold onto the CTS model of instruction, the bad rap we get is likely to continue. We could work harder, teach more closely to the test, and put even more pressure on students, but Cover Test Sort is a model that is not designed to help a large majority of students become proficient learners.

We will continue to make small ineffectual gains at best until we fundamentally restructure our instructional process. **Only a system designed to build competency will develop more competent learners.** Only when we replace CTS with instruction leading to competency will we have significantly more students achieving at high levels, along with developing the qualities of character and the love of learning that are crucial for their futures. Without a new model for teaching and learning, essential content and skills are likely to be "covered" but not well learned. With competency based learning, teachers vigilantly monitor learning and adjust instruction until each student develops essential understandings and skills to competency.

With competency based learning, students travel the path toward essential learning outcomes at their own pace. The key point is that they continue to progress as learners, never disengaging because they became discouraged because of learning frustration and inability to keep up with a pace of instruction designed for someone else. **CBL gives both students and teachers a chance to succeed that is not available within the present system.**

# 8
# Teaching Differently

**"It's my job to deliver the content. It's the students' job to keep up,"** a high school social studies teacher once explained to me with great conviction. As a beginning high school special education teacher, this conversation told me all I needed to know about the support my special needs students would get in his classroom. I recognized that I should avoid placing handicapped learners in this teacher's class, and that many other students would suffer under his instruction.

While this view is incredibly insensitive to the needs of students, it is also consistent with the structure of most curriculum-driven instructional systems. Teachers are given a lot to cover, told that they should be able to use their time well, cover every chapter and content expectation, manage behavior, and somehow motivate kids to try harder so they achieve higher test scores.

> **When covering content is the prime objective, other behaviors suffer: Taking time to build relationships, teaching and practicing classroom routines, helping kids get to know and trust each other, exploring each student's special interests, creating projects and activities which bring learning to life, developing intrinsic motivation to learn, developing values and character.**

Imagine a school bus driver given a route to drive that is much longer and has more stops than could be reasonable managed in the time allowed. In this metaphor, drivers who race through the bus route and get to school on time are given kudos. And if they arrive at school with only a handful of kids, nobody complains.

Many new teachers have been trained to efficiently deliver content and lessons. When they reach the classroom they confront the reality of behavior management, absenteeism, different learning skills, interests, and rates of learning, and the futility of "covering content" when students are not learning. These issues, along with complex school bureaucracies and a lack of professionalism in many school cultures, drives some of our best young educators away from teaching.

> **Learning to become a competency based educator is and will be a challenge. Instead of having one set of lessons to cover, the teacher will understand and respond to the diverse learning needs of her students. Instead of keeping all students on the same page at the same time, students work at their level of readiness. Instead of assuming all students learn in the same way, we recognize the many different ways in which competency might be achieved.**

For those educators who have chosen to stay in our profession, the pressure to cover and the pressure to achieve better test scores has increased year by year. Because Cover Test and Sort is such a pervasive model, many educators don't even consider the alternatives. As we transition to competency based learning, the basic training we provide to teachers will change, on-going professional development will be important, and **we will bring a much needed love of learning back into the schools** and into our lives as professionals.

The rubric for high-quality instruction will change. No longer will the standard include:

- Lesson plans are consistent with the pacing guide and the prescribed GLCEs for each day
- All students are receiving the same prescribed and scripted lesson
- Complete lessons are delivered to all students in the 60-minute standard period

Instead the rubric for high-quality instruction may include:

- Students are working toward essential outcomes at their own instructional level
- Each student can identify the learning outcomes toward which he/she is working
- Students understand what competency for each essential outcomes will look like, and how it can be demonstrated
- Students seek help and support from each other as well as from the teacher
- The classroom is calm, and the students have developed a trusting relationship with teacher and classmates
- The teacher effectively uses formative assessment to adjust instructional plans for each student
- The teacher ensures that each student achieves true competency in every essential skill or step in a learning sequence

**At the secondary level, competency based learning can take many forms.** Within a course-based competency framework, specific competencies for the completion of each course would be clearly defined. Students might test out of some of the specific competencies for each course, use blended learning options, gain experience or skill on the job, or show demonstrations of competency based on summer learning or work experiences.

A competency framework could be based on major areas of study rather than specific courses. These might include science, math, language arts, social science, technology, physical development, and the arts. In some schools, character development could be included as an expected aspect of development.

Minimum standards for graduation/completion would be established, much like the New Hampshire K-12 Science Competencies (2014). Schools, working with students and families, might use varied options for learning to help students meet and exceed these standards.

High schools may collaborate with local employers and colleges to create learning outcome skill sets which align with the needs of local employers. High skill and high pay jobs are a great motivator to keep students on track to achieving the learning goals that establish pathways to earning success within their communities.

Blended learning options will increase based on the availability of quality digital learning programs that can be aligned with student learning goals. Digital learning will support classroom demonstration, and hands-on learning and practice.

> **To work within these competency based learning frameworks, the concept of high school itself may shift away from the identification of a place of learning to the experience of learning, wherever it may occur. Learning may shift away from curriculum silos (English, social studies, science, math), and will certainly shift away from the time-limited systems we currently use.**

**A competency based elementary program** will focus on building all the important learning skills and habits which build the foundation of learning for life. New paradigms require different teaching methodologies and skills.

Rather than using rigid one-size-fits-all pacing guides for the whole class, carefully differentiated instruction occurs frequently throughout the day. Instruction that focuses on crucial learning outcomes students is carefully designed so that student work at their individual instruction level. This can happen within small groups or instructional centers. Digital learning systems support classroom instruction, based on the teacher's assessment of each student's learning needs. Blended learning structures will combine digital and in-person learning.

Peer support and project-based learning can be used to support and integrate student learning.

In a competency based classroom, large group or whole class instruction is used for exploration and enrichment, and for many projects and activities. But large group instruction is not overused when it might create significant learning frustration or boredom for students.

**The importance of having high-quality educators is essential to the use of competency based learning, as teachers do far more than deliver a scripted lesson.** Classroom teachers continually assess student progress and design instructional plans that meet the individual learning needs and instructional levels of their students. This level of professionalism is supported by training and support for teachers in the classroom.

Using a competency based elementary learning system will open up new possibilities for parent involvement in the progress of their children. Parents and teachers working together can give children the practice time needed for proper skill development and accelerate progress on the pathways to high level skill development.

In a competency based elementary classroom, there could be a small but clear set of crucial learning outcomes designed for each grade/age level like the *Essential Skill Inventories PK-3* (Sornson, 2012), usually called a competency framework. For these grade level outcomes, students would get all the time and support needed for the achievement of competency. After meeting these crucial grade-level outcomes, students would proceed to tackle more advanced learning skills and content.

In a competency based elementary classroom, there might also be a master plan for all essential learning steps during the PK and elementary school years. This multi-grade competency framework would define the outcomes and steps within each domain of learning for this developmental phase. **Using this approach, student learning could be carefully tracked accurately even when the student was behind or ahead of grade level skills.**

**The importance of building a safe learning environment** is increased when working within a competency based learning system. **The complexity of knowing each student's learning needs and offering instruction that matches their readiness requires a helping, peaceful, respectful environment to maximize teaching and learning success.** Within that safe learning environment, teachers will develop impeccable classroom routines, teach social skills and self-regulation, and build a community of learners.

The competency based learning classroom looks different than the one-size-fits-all instructional programs we have observed for so long. Using on-going assessment of progress, teachers know exactly which children have achieved proficiency on which skills within the continuum of essential oral language, literacy, social skills, motor skills, numeracy, behavior, and self-regulation skills. Some children may still be working on skills from the previous grade level. Others will be working at grade-level, and still others will be working on skills from a more advanced level. **Proficiency in a skill will only be noted when a student has demonstrated deep understanding of a skill or concept on several occasions, over a period of time, and using several different types of learning materials to ensure both understanding and application.**

Blended learning options will continue to increase and improve, as technology systems and learning programs are further developed. A competency based classroom might have students learning at their individual learning levels in different disciplines at the same time, with some kids working on digital learning while others participate in small groups or center based instruction. Teachers will cultivate the skills that help them create a classroom environment and culture which support this quality of differentiated learning.

**Simpson County School District in rural Mississippi** began implementation of a competency based early learning structure in 2008–09. Using the *Essential Skill Inventories* (Sornson, 2012) in Kindergarten, First, and Second Grade, staff learned to:

- ♦ Clearly identify essential learning outcomes in all the domains of early childhood.

- Use systematic assessment to determine the readiness levels of students in relation to essential outcomes.
- Offer informed instruction and carefully monitor progress until these skills/objectives are deeply understood (competency).
- Allow students to move on to more advanced learning as soon as they are ready.

The district aligned report cards with the *Essential Skill Inventories,* which encouraged staff to help parents understand the concept of crucial learning outcomes and to understand the competencies students were being asked to develop.

As part of an evaluation of improved teacher behaviors based on the use of this competency based learning model, teachers reported significant improvements in their teaching skills and behaviors associated with early learning success (Sornson, 2015).

Simpson County teachers effectively using competency based learning systems reported improvement in their use of systematic formative assessment, with the largest gain reported in their ability to embed assessment into the design of instruction. They described significant improvements in their skills for instructional design, with the largest gains reported in giving some students more time to learn essential skills and re-teaching essential skills until students reach deep understanding.

Teachers also described significant improvements in their skills and behaviors supporting differentiated instruction, and also significant improvements in their ability to understand the learning needs of the whole child.

Teacher perception of changes in their skills and behaviors is supported by changes in student outcomes at Simpson Central School, the pilot school which was the first Mississippi school to begin implementation. Both math and language arts scores have improved significantly on state assessments and this school performance improved from low performing to an A-rated school of excellence.

**Competency based instruction is different than Cover Test and Sort. It offers a different contextual framework for planning and delivering instruction, which will require a different set of teaching skills.**

**University and technical competency based learning options are already proliferating in the U.S.** Employers are clamoring for applicants with the skills need for success on the job, and higher education is responding. On-line and blended options are widely available. The availability of free Massive Open Online Courses (MOOCs) and other digital learning options add energy to this change. Individual universities or departments are developing competency based learning models following the models of engineering and medical schools that have long held standards for competency.

Around the world, nations have begun the transformation to more efficient and personalized systems of adult learning. School to work programs, technical certificate programs, and degree programs recognize the need to have outcomes that matter, and are reshaping their learning options. Competency based learning can be designed within a course-based framework, in which specific competencies for the completion of each course would be clearly defined. Or a degree program can define exit outcomes, assess student needs and design a learning plan that helps students develop the required competencies. Students might test out of some of the specific competencies for each course or program, use blended learning options, gain experience or skill on the job, or show demonstrations of competency based on summer learning or work experiences.

Within a competency based post-secondary learning program, the pace of learning can vary, with some students more quickly moving along the skill pathways that lead to crucial exit outcomes. Even the learning experiences might vary, with some students responding better to classroom instruction while others learn better on the job with hands-on learning options. But the outcomes for learning are clear and constant, and once those essential learning outcomes are achieved, the student receives the certificates or degrees which they have earned.

> **High quality CBL educators will:**
>
> - use formative and summative assessment to understand the learning skills and needs of each student
> - allow students to work unrushed within a viable instructional plan
> - teach crucial skills at the student's level of readiness
> - differentiate instruction based on student learning needs
> - use systematic formative assessment to monitor progress

**No amount of tweaking to the assembly line Cover Test Sort model will adequately meet the learning needs of our future.** Better outcomes will come **only after we shift to a systems model for learning** that accelerates individual learning while also creating a more joyful and productive classroom environment.

The competency based classroom teacher will be a well-trained and highly skilled professional educator, able to identify crucial outcomes, assess student learning needs, and differentiate instruction toward the development of competency. The competency based classroom teacher will build a culture of respect and safety in which students can work at their best learning level with confidence and joy. The CBL classroom teacher will know her students, understand their learning skills, learning preferences, and learning interests as she works to help students be successful learners and fall in love with learning for life.

We are stepping into a new age, in which educators will be valued professionals rather than drones delivering instruction for all according to the pacing guide. **These men and women will unlock the potential of our students and our nation, and must be regarded as some of the most valued professionals in our society.**

# 9

# Systems Thinking for Competency Based Learning

**In the old Cover Sort Test systems model,** teachers were given a set of books, or a curriculum, and asked to "cover" the material. For good teachers, this job included building relationships, making content meaningful whenever possible, and managing behavior in the classroom. In recent years, pacing guides became a greater part of daily life for teachers and students, creating an unrelenting pace of instruction that took time away from the non-content duties of a good classroom teacher.

**In the competency based learning model teachers respond daily to a different set of expectations.** First, they identify and work with a set of clear learning objectives that are associated with long-term success in a domain of learning or in the application of knowledge and skills. This set of crucial learning outcomes is often referred to as a competency framework. Second, teachers assess student readiness for instruction so that they can determine which skills/knowledge are already in place, which are developing, and which are not yet developed at all. With a solid understanding of the competency framework and student readiness, teachers have a clear view of student learning needs and readiness. Third, teachers plan and deliver instruction based on their understanding of student learning needs. Instruction can be significantly different for individual students based on their learning needs. Throughout this process great teachers will develop relationships, establish positive classroom routines, manage behavior, make learning meaningful, and understand the needs of the whole child as an essential part of building learners for life.

Instead of relying on Cover-Test-Sort as we have in the past, **in a competency based learning model the assumptions shift to identification of crucial learning outcomes, assessing student readiness, and then delivering instruction to match student readiness.**

## Identify Crucial Learning Outcomes

It all starts with clear learning goals. With a small set of clearly defined crucial outcomes, a clear pathway to competency, and a goal of competency for every child, teachers work within a different system designed to produce far more competent learners.

**If you ran a coffee shop,** every new barista would be trained to meet your expectations for good service and good coffee. These expectations might include how to greet customers, basic interpersonal skills, coffee knowledge, technical skills for making products, handling money and credit, and having a working knowledge of your shop and your products. A successful owner/manager would identify these outcomes as specifically as possible, with the goal of training new employees for as long as needed to achieve full competency and consistency.

**If you worked within a community coalition to help more high school students develop skills that would prepare them to work for a successful local employer,** you would determine which jobs were available and likely to remain viable for some time in the future, and the set of skills that would allow students to get these jobs and succeed for many years to come. Then you would work backwards, building a scaffold of skills that must be solidly in place to reach the skill outcomes that will determine success.

**If you worked as a kindergarten mathematics teacher,** at the very least you would identify the crucial math skills that prepare students to be fully ready for first grade math. This would become your small set of essential outcomes for kindergarten math learning:

- Demonstrates counting to 100
- Has one-to-one correspondence for numbers 1 to 30
- Understands combination (to 10)
- Recognizes number groups without counting (2 to 10)

Better yet, you would determine the sequence of skills that build a full foundation of solid math skills during the PK to Grade 3 early childhood years, so that you could identify your students' math skills at present, fill in any gaps in their knowledge/skills from previous grades, and allow them to move forward to more challenging skills once they fully establish competency in the essential Kindergarten math skills.

**Contrast this with standard practice in most schools.** Each year, teachers are expected to "cover" hundreds of grade level content standards, give a little extra attention to high priority skills that are more likely to be included in the state mandated assessments, while keeping up with the pacing guide. The idea that we are racing through instruction, covering too much and covering it poorly, is not new!

*Students learn more when we teach less—but teach it well* (Dempster, 1993).

*The tendency toward overload is strong in schools—and crippling to improvement efforts* (Fullan & Hargreaves, 1996).

*Although U.S. mathematics textbooks attempt to address 175% more topics than do German textbooks and 350% more topics than do Japanese textbooks, both German and Japanese students significantly outperform U.S. students in mathematics. Similarly, although U.S. science textbooks attempt to cover 930% more topics than do German textbooks and 433% more topics than do Japanese textbooks, both German and Japanese students significantly outperform U.S. students in science achievement as well* (Schmidt et al., 1996).

*We will realize the promise of school reform when we establish standards and expectations for reaching them that are clear, not confusing; essential, not exhaustive. The result will be a new coherence and a shared focus that could be the most propitious step we can take toward educating all students well* (Schmoker & Marzano, 1999).

**Thoughtful educators have been calling for a clearer and narrower instructional focus for decades.**

*The National Mathematics Advisory Panel recommends that math curriculum should include fewer topics, spending enough time to make sure each is learned in enough depth that it need not be revisited in later grades* (National Mathematics Advisory Counsel, 2008).

The Professional Learning Community (PLC) model developed by Rick DuFour, Bob Eaker, and Becky DuFour et al. (1998, 2016) focuses on four critical questions:

- What do we expect students to learn?
- How do we know when they have learned it?
- How will we respond when students don't learn?
- How will we respond when students have learned?

# Notice that Step One in this PLC Model does not ask what must be Covered. Instead it asks what must be Learned!

At the conclusion of his work, *Visible Learning* (2009), John Hattie synthesized hundreds of educational research studies over several decades and concluded that the most powerful strategy for improving student learning occurs when teachers work together in collaborative teams to collectively complete the following tasks:

- Clarify what student must learn.
- Gather evidence of student learning.
- Analyze evidence of student learning.
- Identify the most effective teaching strategies.

> It all starts with clear learning goals. With a small set of clearly defined crucial outcomes, and a clear pathway to competency, and a goal of competency for every child, teachers will work within a system designed to produce far more competent learners. Clear learning goals provide the objective toward which we will work until the job is done.

**Unfortunately,** our prevalent model for instruction still focuses on what gets covered instead of what gets learned. Not only have we held onto the coverage model in most schools, but the content we so vigorously cover does not begin to prepare most students for the skills of collaboration, self-regulation, empathy, technology, and problem-solving that most good jobs demand today.

**Fortunately,** both inside and outside or K-12 educations systems, change is brewing. As far back as 1991 U.S. Secretary of Labor Lynn Martin convened the Secretary's Commission on Achieving Necessary Skills (SCANS), asking an esteemed committee to define the skills needed for employment, propose acceptable levels of proficiency, suggest effective ways to assess proficiency, and develop a dissemination strategy for the nation's schools, businesses, and homes.

Their report described both foundation skills and competencies needed for workplace success. Even though this commission completed its work decades ago, its recommendations are a clear voice for a focus on developing competencies needed for success at work and in life (National Technical Information Service, 1991).

In the ever-growing and changing world of technology, Microsoft, Oracle, Cisco, Apple, Google, Ubuntu, Skillable, and other providers offer professional certifications for those who complete training and demonstrate competency in a clearly articulated set of skill expectations. Each certification is specific to one set of skills. Advanced certifications rely on the development of a progression of skills sets, a pathway to higher level skills. Only with competency in each required skill is a certificate earned.

In the world of vocational and technical training, clear learning outcomes are the norm rather than an exception. Electricians are expected to show competency in a specific set of skills to be licensed as master electrician, journeyman electrician, residential wireman, maintenance electrician, or electrical contractor. These could be considered end-goal competencies, requirements for certification or employment.

In 2013, as part of its competency based learning initiative, the New Hampshire State Board of Education approved college and career ready competencies in Mathematics and English Language Arts. Science competencies were added in 2014. Since then a broader framework of graduation competencies has been established in New Hampshire, with other states studying and moving in this same direction. With these end-goals in mind, educators are building a careful sequence of learning steps for which competency is the standard.

**End-goals are not enough** for a competency based system of learning. There must also be carefully developed **pathways to competency,** which describe all the steps needed to achieve crucial entry-outcomes to a profession, or graduation competencies, or any exit set of exit outcomes. These pathways clearly describe all the building blocks needed to achieve the high-level learning skills so needed in the world today.

A competency pathway is focused on student learning outcomes, and is built with the following design principles in mind:

- Students advance upon mastery, not age.
- The pathway is built with explicit and measurable learning objectives.
- Assessment is primarily formative, and skills or concepts are assessed in multiple contexts to guarantee both deep understanding and application.

**Competency based pathways rely on a sequence of explicit learning goals,** allowing students to work at the appropriate level of challenge, and progress to the next level of challenge as soon as they are completely ready. Crucial learning goals can be stated as end-goals, but a competency based pathway is comprised of the many crucial learning goals which lead to a sought after end- goal.

Pathways to competency can take different forms. Medical school and Navy Seal training offer explicit end-goal competencies, and stages and skills in the development of those competencies, but with the clear expectation that not all candidates will complete the training.

The Khan Academy and other web-based learning platforms offer step-by-step learning objectives leading to higher level outcomes. Students can take as much time as needed to work on each learning goal. When proficiency is achieved, the next goals become available to the learner.

A competency pathway could include a set of crucial outcomes taught as a course. For some students competency could be achieved by taking the course once. For other students, it might take more than one time to achieve competency in the required outcomes. Using this type of structure, in which some students are likely to take the course again, it would serve students better if only a small set of outcomes were taught as one unit, to avoid the need for students to repeat a whole semester or year of learning.

A high school biology class might include a competency structure in which a set of crucial outcomes are identified, and all students are expected to achieve proficiency in these outcomes.

In addition to the basic competencies there might be a set of higher level competencies for some of the students in the class, but which are not considered essential for course completion.

*Essential Math Skills* (Sornson, 2014) offers a competency based math structure for the Preschool to Grade 3 years. It describes the 29 foundation skills that are essential for long-term math learning success during these early childhood years.

These are the skills that merit continuous monitoring and development until they are completely proficient.

The *Essential Math Skills PK to Grade 3* framework provides a multi-age set of crucial learning outcomes, and it can also be used to identify the skills that serve as essential outcomes for particular grade. For example, Kindergarten math programs focusing on these four essential math skills would prepare far more students who are fully ready for typical First Grade math instruction.

| *Kindergarten* | *Intervention* | *Developing* | *Proficient* |
|---|---|---|---|
| **Demonstrates counting to 100** | Counts to less than 20 with accuracy | Able to count to 50 to 99 with accuracy | Counts to 100 with accuracy |
| **Has one-to-one correspondence for numbers 1 to 30** | Can count fewer than 10 objects with one-to-one correspondence | Shows one-to-one correspondence when counting 10 to 29 objects | Shows one-to-one correspondence when counting 30 or more objects |
| **Understands combination (to 10)** | Does not consistently understand how to add on or take away 1–3 objects without recounting | Consistently adds on or takes away 1–3 objects without recounting | Adds on or takes-away from a set of objects without recounting (1–10) |
| **Recognizes number groups without counting (2 to 10)** | Recognizes number groups of 1 or 2 without counting | Recognizes number groups of 3 to 5 without counting | Recognizes number groups up to 10 without counting individual objects |

This narrow focus on four math learning outcomes in Kindergarten is not intended to be a complete math curriculum or program, which should be designed to include projects, activities, extensions, and content. But it does provide a focus for learning, derived from the experiences of many teachers and researchers, showing which outcomes are crucial to long-term math learning success.

The *Essential Math Skills Inventory, PreK to Grade 3* (Sornson, 2014), provides a broader framework for identifying skills at each level so that, if needed, a student can go back to a previous grade level to catch up on essential skills that were not fully learned, or progress to a more advanced level of skills if she is ready. Using this system, some Kindergarten students may need to focus on learning crucial Preschool-level skills:

- (Pre-K) Demonstrates one-to-one correspondence for numbers 1–10, with steps
- (Pre-K) Demonstrates one-to-one correspondence for numbers 1–10, with manipulatives
- (Pre-K) Adds on using numbers 1–10, with steps
- (Pre-K) Adds on using numbers 1–10, with manipulatives

Other student would be fully ready for K level math learning outcomes:

- (K) Demonstrates counting to 100
- (K) Has one-to-one correspondence for numbers 1–30
- (K) Understands combinations (to 10)
- (K) Recognizes number groups without counting (2–10)

While still other students would likely be ready for First Grade learning outcomes:

- Counts objects with accuracy to 100
- Replicates visual or movement patterns
- Understands concepts of add on or take away (to 30)
- Adds/subtracts single digit problems on paper
- Shows a group of objects by number (to 100)

In Kennewick, Washington, as reported in *Annual Growth for All Students, Catch Up Growth for Those Who Are Behind* (Fielding et al., 2007), the school district identified a sequence of skill levels for the development of phonemic awareness, phonics, accuracy, fluency, and comprehension. Using a process of formative assessment, progress in these aspects of literacy development was carefully monitored, and students were then given instruction and practice time for each skill until it was mastered.

*The Pre-K to Grade 3 Essential Skill Inventories* (Sornson, 2012) are based on a competency based structure for each of the domains of early childhood. Progress on the crucial skills for **oral language, phonological skills, literacy, numeracy, sensory-motor, behavior, and self-regulation skills** are monitored systematically to ensure that each child is given the time and support needed for the development of proficiency in each skill of each domain. In a competency based early childhood classroom, some students would be expected to be working on grade level, while others would be completing work from previous levels or advancing to the level typically associated with the next grade.

Competency based learning frameworks require a different way of thinking about teaching and learning. Without the primary directive to "cover content" at the same rate for all students, we are faced with the challenge of defining specific learning pathways leading to crucial competencies, and then delivering instruction at each students individual level as they progress along the pathways toward skills that matter. It begins with understanding each student's readiness for learning before delivering instruction that keeps each student in a high success zone that encourages motivation and learning success.

## Assess Student Readiness for Learning

For good reasons, **most teachers are sick and tired** of all the time and effort put into state-mandated standardized assessments. Committees design the curriculum to align with the impossible task of adequately "covering" the grade level content objectives that will be included in the grade level standardized assessments. Then teachers race through the curriculum in an effort to get it all covered, often neglecting the importance of building classroom routines, building relationships with students, building a positive classroom culture, and taking advantage of moments of opportunity that might allow deeper learning of content or social-emotional situations that emerge during the busy weeks of instruction.

Then there are the many hours of explicit test preparation, followed by the weeks of delivering the state standardized assessments. Most teachers resent and are discouraged by the time and effort put into this standardized assessment of all their students, which offers data that quantitatively tracks classroom and school learning outcomes.

Standardized assessment has some real value, which will be explored more carefully later in this chapter. But standardized assessment data could be collected far more efficiently, without the immense time commitment used in our present system.

> **Assessment for learning is underused and undervalued in most American classrooms.**

**What's usually missing is assessment for learning.** Standardized testing is not constructed or implemented in a way that gives teachers the information to shape instruction on a daily or weekly basis to meet the needs of their students. Assessment for learning is usually called formative assessment. It can be used to formulate a plan for instruction that meets the needs of students.

Amazingly, many teachers have little direct training in using formative assessment for planning daily or weekly instruction. For all the wonderful books about the interaction between formative assessment and differentiated instruction (Carol Ann Tomlinson, Robert Marzano, etc.), the pacing guide-driven system in most schools doesn't allow much variation from the one-size-fits-all plan for curriculum implementation.

Over the years, many teachers have expressed frustration when it comes to their lack of authority/permission to vary the instructional plan to better meet the needs of their students. In math, early elementary teachers have emotionally explained to me that they absolutely know that a large group of students, often a majority of students, are not ready for the content they are expected to cover this week. Middle school teachers have shaken their heads at the mere idea that they might be allowed to go back and fill in the gaps in understanding they see in their students. Imagine being a teacher of math, science, literature, or anything else that is built on a progression of skills, seeing a classroom full of blank, frustrated, or disengaged students, and nonetheless proceeding to cover the curriculum as if they might be ready to learn.

Formative assessment can take many shapes. A pretest before beginning a chapter or unit could tell you which students have the foundation skills needed for success, which students might have already learned the content you are getting ready to cover, and which students need to learn foundational vocabulary or skills that would raise the odds for successful learning.

A competency framework would give teachers a running record of which skills have been fully learned for every student in your class, and offer a great look at which kids need small groups or intensive support before beginning a new area of instruction.

Simple observation is by far my favorite brand of formative assessment. By offering an instructional activity and carefully observing student engagement, an experienced teacher can usually see which kids are ready and able for this level of difficulty.

If I give my three-year-old granddaughter a puzzle that is too difficult, a few moments of observation are all it takes to see that I need to find an easier puzzle. When teaching young child to throw and catch, or ride a bike, we all use observational formative assessment to set the right level of difficulty for this task. A little bit challenging, but not too much, is the ancient formula.

In a very few schools, teachers or support staff are trained to develop a comprehensive profile on the strengths and needs of each student, including language development, literacy, numeracy, nearpoint visual skills, auditory processing skills, motor skills, self-regulation and social emotional skills, along with content skills. With this profile, they can readily understand the needs of each student as they plan instruction for the classroom that meets the needs of individual students.

With a good sense of what each student can do, we can look for ways to adjust the difficulty of instruction. Sometimes that means reducing the quantity of learning goals (i.e. spelling words or math problems), or letting some students work in a center or small group to build necessary vocabulary for the upcoming lesson, or develop project based learning that allows more advanced students to interact with students who need support and encouragement.

In any high functioning competency based classroom, **the teacher will spend a large part of everyday carefully observing students** so she can match instruction to the needs of each student.

## Planning and Delivering Instruction to Meet Students' Needs

Scripted and rigidly paced learning programs be warned. Your time is up. The coverage-driven one-size-fits-all learning model cannot be saved. Parents would never use this model to teach their children to catch a ball, or ride a bike, or drive a car. Soon parents and educators will realize it must not be used on their children for other crucial learning outcomes, like reading and writing, science, and math.

The CTS system of instruction has overwhelming limitations. Some students need more time to learn important content. Some students don't have the prerequisite skills, and really need to step back and fill in the gaps of important learning sequences. Other students already know the material, and are bored. Some students have been sick for a few days and out of school, and others have challenges outside of school and can't concentrate in the classroom.

**The challenge and opportunity for schools and educators** is to learn a new way of teaching in which students and teachers find much greater success, respect, confidence, and joy. **So look around. Competency based learning systems are all around us.** Our doctors, pilots, electricians, and tech companies are using competency based learning systems, with clearly defined learning outcomes and the requirement to demonstrate competency. In our communities there are gymnastics, martial arts, and scouting programs which have longstanding traditions of progress based on demonstrated competency. Digital learning systems abound. More and more universities offer competency based programs.

**Imagine teaching a high school Biology class** in which a small set of crucial content and skill competencies have been identified, along with a competency framework that identifies all the prerequisite skills that lead toward these crucial Biology outcomes. The required outcomes for this class have been clearly defined, then also modeled.

Teachers have worked with the students to accurately understand where they stand on the pathways to these required Bio outcomes. The assessment process was blended into projects and activities that provided good opportunities to show Bio knowledge, and also the problem-solving and collaboration skills that are part of the broader vision of competencies for your school. With a good understanding of their students, teachers devised small group, large group, and blended learning activities that allowed them to group students for optimal learning, sometimes with students at their level, and sometimes in mixed level groups.

After a while, students got the understanding that learning essential skills is not a race. Some students were able to move ahead to more advanced concepts and skills, while others needed more time to establish foundational skills needed to become proficient in the identified essential outcomes. Teachers kept track, carefully noting every learning gain toward the essential outcomes for this course, but also noticing which kids needed another try or a different approach to gaining skills. As professionals, teachers knew that is was their job to figure out how to maximize progress for each student rather than follow a script for each lesson.

**Imagine a middle school math class,** in which specific math skills have been identified as the crucial outcomes for sixth grade. Most of the class is ready to work on these skills, but will progress at different rates. Some students are way behind, and lack deep understanding of skills going back to second grade.

Other students are ahead, and are ready for skills typically taught in seventh or eighth grade.

In a competency based math learning system, the teacher will use formative assessment to understand the needs of each student within the structure of essential math skills. Demonstration, peer tutoring, blended learning, small group lessons, and digital resources like the Khan Academy are among the instructional options available to the teacher, as she **monitors progress toward the crucial outcomes and plans instruction to meet the needs of her students.**

On any given day, the teacher may offer a demonstration, work with two different small groups, supervise students who are working on Khan Academy lessons, and have a few students who travel to another class to participate in higher level instruction. Students spend significant minutes each day learning and practicing math at their level of readiness. Because students are experiencing success each day, motivation is good, and discipline problems are few. Group activities and class beginning and ending routines help create a positive community climate, and contribute to language, social, and collaboration skills.

**Imagine an elementary school** in which both grade level crucial competencies and age-range pathways to competency have been established in all the domains of development. Teachers know the skill levels of each child in language, literacy, numeracy, motor skills, social and self-regulation skills. The curriculum map ensures "coverage" of key grade-level concepts, but coverage is not the end-goal. Teachers are expected to know their students, **and vigilantly monitor progress toward crucial grade level outcomes.**

Teachers design instruction so that students are exposed to general concepts and also have time to develop essential skills at students' specific levels of readiness, whatever that might be. Instructional level, student interests, required curriculum, essential learning outcomes, and the social dynamic of each class are considered by the teacher as she designs instruction for each upcoming week.

By knowing each student and offering **big doses of learning at level,** student learning gains are optimized. By carefully monitoring progress, the teacher knows if progress has stalled in any learning domain. If so, she collaborates with colleagues and experiments with any factors which might be the critical piece to help this student get back on track. **Constantly monitoring, constantly adjusting instruction,** this teacher is a high-quality high-skill professional.

**Imagine a preschool** in which the teacher has a high-quality curriculum framework and also monitors progress toward crucial kindergarten readiness skills in oral language, literacy, number sense, visual motor skills, gross motor skills, behavior, and self-care. Each week she **monitors progress** in at least two of these domains of early childhood, and each week she **plans instruction based on a clear understanding of student learning needs.**

As important as any learning outcome, this preschool teacher also builds a culture for connection and learning. Children are safe and happy, challenged but never overwhelmed. In this classroom, the foundation for learning for life is being built, and this CBL preschool teacher will never let a child begin to believe that his efforts aren't good enough, or that he'll never be good at math, or that learning is boring and hard. She has a framework of skills in each domain, a set of outcomes that correspond with full Kindergarten readiness, and the time to assess each child and deliver instruction at that child's level of readiness.

**Imagine a university which offers both certificates and degrees.** Each certificate and each degree program has established **minimum competencies for completion.** For these knowledge and skill competencies, there are no grades. There is only competency. You can take a course or engage in a learning activity **as many times as necessary to learn what you need to become competent.**

At this university, if you have already developed a competency on the job, in a previous course, or through independent learning, you are not asked to retake courses to revisit that skill or content. Assessment systems identify where each student is at on the continuum of skills leading to the skills required for a certificate or degree.

Degree programs include more than just the set of minimum competencies determined by the university. They also include **a personal design for learning,** a set of skill and content outcomes **which the student has chosen** as important, in combination with the minimum competencies expected for the degree. The university is then a partner in helping define learning pathways which will lead to the competencies that support your plan for your future.

> As we move toward a competency based learning framework, there are incredible opportunities for enterprising educators. New learning delivery systems which are not confined to the structure of a time-limited course, and new assessment systems to track progress toward competency are already being devised. Digital systems for learning are just one piece of this new paradigm for learning. Teachers will develop project based, community based, and collaborative designs for developing competency that focuses on the development of the whole child, preparing students for life.

**There are many models from which we can learn** as we develop options in every community in every state and every nation. The **Khan Academy** has developed a "Constellation of Math Skills", which displays the relationships between math skills, and from which a pathway from basic math to higher order skills can be inferred. All good digital learning systems control progress based on the development of foundation skills needed for ongoing learning success.

In early math development, the *Essential Math Skills* (Sornson, 2014) shows a progression of crucial skills from preschool to grade three, along with many movement and manipulative based activities to develop each skill to deep understanding. Various digital math learning programs are built upon a progression of skills, which in digital format can be carefully tracked for progress toward competency.

In the crucial early childhood years (preschool through grade three) there are skills in oral language, reading, phonologic skills, writing, motor skills, numeracy, social, and self-regulation skills, which are crucial for the experience of early learning success, and therefore crucial to establish a healthy learning trajectory for life. Using a manageable set of crucial outcomes for these years the ***Essential Skill Inventories Pk to Grade 3*** (Sornson, 2012) give teachers discrete learning outcomes for each grade, but also a sequence of skills that allow each student to be given instruction at the right instructional level to maximize learning and avoid disengagement.

In New Hampshire, the State Board of Education has established **college and career ready outcome standards for ELA, Math and Science.** Along with clear competency expectations for graduation, they have also developed a structure of recommended content and process standards for required high school coursework.

Digital learning programs like **Luminosity** develop cognitive skills including speed, memory, attention, problem-solving, and flexibility (http://brain-games-puzzle-stores-review.topten reviews.com/lumosity-review.html). The program carefully monitors progress, and adjusts the rate of difficulty, so that students are challenged but never frustrated to the point of disengagement.

**VINCI** is an early childhood focused company whose game-based learning systems tracks progress, offers activities in the student's instructional zone, and gradually tiers instruction to higher levels of competency in language, math and science.

**Western Governor's University** was founded in 1997, and offered a self-paced, personalized, on-line learning program to meet the needs of adults who did not have the time or access to a traditional university experience. WGU has served as a model and a catalyst for the many universities now offering some version of competency based learning.

> **The most important innovations in competency based learning are still waiting to happen in classrooms and schools across the nation. Our work has just begun.**

For most of us, with our personal experiences growing up in Cover Test Sort schools, being trained using CTS standards, and working as educators within the typical CTS school structure, learning new skills for competency based learning will be a challenge. **In a competency based system it will be far more important that educators have well-developed skills for formative assessment, understanding the needs of the whole child, differentiated instruction, working with parents, developing a culture of personal responsibility for learning, and professional collaboration.**

In our present system it is entirely possible for a teacher to "cover" a unit or chapter without carefully understanding the learning needs of his students. Some teachers find the coverage model comfortable, and will resist changing to a model that requires more knowledge of each student and more ability to differentiate instruction. Helping teachers understand this new model for learning, and develop skills to support high-quality competency based learning, will take the steady leadership of administrators and teacher leaders. Developing initiatives to help teachers become "competent" in the skills to support CBL will require professional development and teacher assessment systems much different than those which are typical today.

**High quality competency based learning will depend on professional collaboration** in schools. The complexity of understanding and responding to the needs of individual learners demands the benefits of teamwork. Developing new systems, procedures, conversations, and skills will take a learning community, a living model of the collaborative learning community we want for our students.

**Professional Learning Community** (PLC) offers an effective model in which educators work collectively to ensure high levels of student learning. This collaboration will be crucial to the development of schools and programs in which all staff offer high-quality competency based learning.

Developed by Rick DuFour, Bob Eaker, and Becky DuFour (1998, 2016), PLCs focus on four critical questions for disciplined innovation:

- What do we expect students to learn?
- How do we know when they have learned it?
- How will we respond when students don't learn?
- How will we respond when students have learned?

**School administrators will take on different roles** in a competency based learning system. Managing a CTS system includes enforcing pacing guides, providing security for state assessments, spending countless hours evaluating teachers, defending test scores to the public, working with unhappy parents, enforcing discipline with students who are frustrated or bored, and trying to find a few minutes to build relationships and provide instructional leadership.

**In a competency based system, with its emphasis on personalized learning and clear outcomes,** effective leaders will act as coaches, build professional learning groups, help develop pathways to competency for both students and staff, support differentiated instruction, develop the culture and climate for effective learning and teaching, and build professional routines which support the process of helping every child follow the pathways that lead to competency. The transition to competency will require leaders who can work with others, hold to a clear vision of a new learning model, continue to be open to learning, build networks of collaboration, and be the calm voice of change.

**Disciplined innovation** is an essential ingredient of successful education in a competency based learning system. Both teachers and administrators will be constantly learning, understanding the learning needs of students and experimenting to find materials and methods that match the learning readiness, skills, and interests of students. There is no more One Best Way.

With clear learning outcomes in mind, and with a careful awareness of the needs of each student, the competency based teacher develops a teaching/learning plan, implements her learning plan, and then uses formative assessment to discover that it worked better for some students than for others. Every day you plan, deliver instruction, observe and assess, and come up with ideas to improve instruction tomorrow.

Some students need more time, and the disciplined innovator figures a way to give them more time. Some students develop proficiency in a skill far more quickly than expected, and the disciplined innovator moves those students forward to more challenging skills and content.

Some students don't respond well at all to the instructional plan. It's a miss. Rather than blame those students, the disciplined teacher-innovator considers other ways to teach every crucial concept or skill. Whatever it takes. Any amount of time, in or out of school, in groups or on a screen, using paper or using manipulatives, the disciplined innovator finds a way to help students learn.

> **Helping each child progress on the path to clear learning goals requires disciplined instructional innovation based on actionable data every single day.**

**Successful competency-focused educators** will plan instruction with the understanding that for every crucial outcome, competency takes precedence over coverage. Teachers will devise pathways to competency, carefully monitor progress, modify instruction to fit student readiness, and give students all the time needed to achieve learning success. Administrators will build a culture for learning for staff, students, and parents. Highly skilled professional educators, with and in-depth understanding of each student and with skills in formative assessment and differentiated instruction, will create classrooms and programs where learning comes alive.

# 10

# Whole Child Competency

"Just tell us what's going to be on the test, so we know what to study," is a common refrain in many schools.

In CTS schools students are told what's worth learning. Content is delivered in a time-limited format. A test will determine how well they learned it. Some students are overwhelmed and confused by the content. Some students are incredibly bored. Some students don't have the underlying skills or knowledge needed to be highly successful in this subject no matter how hard they try. Some students disengage from learning and just show up, hoping that they might somehow magically pass the test and get a credit. For all of them it will be the same test. Then each student receives a grade. Then we move on.

> **In most schools, students are told what to learn and then extrinsically motivated by grades, credits, class rank, status, and admission to college. High-stakes testing has added pressure to the system, making pacing guides more rigid and district assessment schedules more aggressive. This system design is deeply troubling if you recognize the importance of self- initiated learning in the information age.**

In a world where lifelong learning was a privilege to be enjoyed by only a few men and women, the CTS design worked well enough. Since we are now living in a world in which new information and new technology are constantly changing the demands of the workplace, the CTS design is doing incredible harm by causing many students to disengage from learning and other students to expect that learning should be easy.

**Successful learners in the information age must be curious and excited about learning.** Effective learners will have the habits of mind that allow them to gather information, pose clear theories, investigate, persist, collaborate, critically review, and change ideas based on new information. **In the other-directed learning environment of a Cover Test and Sort school, the emphasis is far more on compliance and completion than on self-regulation and intrinsic motivation to learn.**

The importance of self-regulation for successful lifelong learning offers a good example of how important it is to use a whole child perspective when planning competency based learning. Self- regulation begins with the development of self-calming, focusing, persisting, delaying gratification, and adjusting your emotional, physical, and attentional state to meet the needs of your situation. As students develop basic self-regulation skills, they become calm enough on the inside to look outside of themselves and notice the lives and feelings of others. This is the beginning of empathy, which is a foundation for the development of social skills and social-emotional intelligence. **The capacity to self-regulate for both social and academic learning is among the best predictors of who will become successful in school, in work, and in life.**

A three-decade-long study in New Zealand (Moffitt T., et al, 2011) looking at more than 1000 young people showed that children with low self-regulation are:

- More likely to smoke, have health problems, and bad credit.
- 3x more likely to commit a crime.
- 3x more likely to have multiple addictions.
- 2x more likely to be single parents.

As reported by Angela Duckworth (2007) and others, self-regulation contributes to the development of resilience and character. In Walter Mischel's famous Marshmallow Experiment, a researcher offered four-year-old children a marshmallow. The researcher offered each child a choice. On the desk was a bell. She was going to leave the room, and the child could ring the bell at any time and eat one marshmallow on her return. But if the child waited for the researcher to return on her own after 15 minutes, the child would get two marshmallows instead of one.

Mischel (1989) tracked the academic progress of these students over time, and the correlation between the child's wait time and later academic success was significant. Many years after, children who waited for 15 minutes had **SAT scores which were on average 210 points higher** than those of children who rang the bell after only 30 seconds. The capacity to self-regulate, whether by an ability to distract themselves or delay gratification, had contributed to the development of the learning skills measured on this college entry exam.

**In a well-devised competency based learning system, self-regulation and intrinsic motivation to learn will be among the crucial outcomes to help students become successful lifelong learners.**

In classrooms across America today there are students who are frustrated and others who are bored. The frustrated kids try, fail, and begin to shut down. They learned that effort and persistence are not enough, and they become disengaged learners who seldom practice using focus, persistence, inquiry, or reflection in the classroom.

The bored kids know that they can pass most tests with minimal effort, so they tune out. Someone else chose a set of learning outcomes that seem unconnected to each other or to life. Without much challenge, without any personal connection to the material, and without clear goals to reach, the process of learning is dull. They tune out, ask questions like "What do I have to study to pass this test?" or "What do I need to get a B?"

FIGURE 10.1 Student Motivation

**Competency based learning is not just about learning typical academic content at a more individualized pace.** In a well-designed competency based learning system far more students will develop patterns of self-initiated learning, skills for self-regulation, collaboration, and problem-solving. They will develop skills that help them focus, sustain effort, work with others, and solve-problems in ways that are not possible within the course and content models we are using today. Far more students will understand that effort and application bring learning rewards, embrace the challenge, and choose to learn.

With clear and meaningful learning goals, instead of frustration leading to avoiding learning, more students will embrace learning. At home, on weekends, in the summer we will see students choose to make progress on the pathways that lead to important outcome competencies. **Any time, any place, any pace learning** will become more prevalent as students buy-in to learning goals that will truly make a difference in their lives.

The lack of joyful self-initiated learning builds patterns of disengagement and lassitude which are destructive to the patterns that modern kids need to succeed. Competency based learning programs, starting as they must with a clear statement of essential learning goals, must include an awareness of the whole developing student, including academic, social-emotional, self-discipline, artistic, and movement skills that will help students become healthy and confident adults. And successful programs will include a strong emphasis on student choice as part of the selection of learning goals and curriculum.

**If our goal is to help far more students become successful learners for life,** we must design classrooms and schools that are far less top-down in the development of learning goals and curriculum, along with learning environments that work for the mix of small group learning, individual support, whole class instruction, digital learning, project based learning, and community based learning. We will need learning environments in which students are calm, focused, self-regulated, flexible, and ready to learn. Safe and positive classroom and school cultures will be a necessary part of this evolution.

During the past few decades, however, in many schools we've moved further away from the careful development of safety, trust, and relationships as part of classroom management.

"I used to take time to build connections with my students," many teachers have explained to me, "but there is just not time for that anymore." In the rush to cover more content and do more test- prep, teachers have done what they felt they must. Time to get to know each student, help students get to know the teacher, carefully teach classroom procedures, practice procedures until they became routines, and helping students get to know and trust each other has been surrendered to the district pacing guides.

Under the guise of coverage-driven rigor, many classrooms have become unsafe environments for students, places where:

- ♦ Students compete with each other for better grades rather than collaborate in support of one another.
- ♦ Students might be ridiculed by other students or by the teacher.

- Attention is given to the things you do wrong.
- Your mistakes are called to the attention of others.
- Your weaker skills are easily exposed.
- Student misbehavior is tolerated rather than taking the time to deal with it effectively.
- There is little time available for building positive social skills, emotional intelligence, or relationships with others.

> **In the pursuit of better testing outcomes, schools have chosen rigorous curriculum expectations over the importance of classroom culture, relationships, trust, play, character building, and social-emotional learning. It's ironic because we have neglected the conditions for learning which might lead to better testing outcomes.**

Highly anxious or insecure students don't learn well, and our present CTS system is creating anxiety for our kids at a record pace. During the Covid-19 years, even more children identified as anxious about their ability to learn and showed less intrinsic motivation to learn. As we move to competency based learning models, we have the opportunity to build classrooms and learning programs that are much more respectful and joyful, and which also help to produce better learning results for more students.

The deliberate planning of safe, secure, trusting classroom and school cultures will not only benefit the learning rates of children. We should also consider the school culture and its impact on staff as we begin our transition into competency based learning. If we expect educators to be engaged in continuous professional learning and thoughtful problem-solving, school culture matters.

> **A student who feels safe is more able to be calm and focused and more likely to persist and delay gratification. With this pattern of self-regulation skills well-developed, a student is more able to develop empathy, resilience, social skills and emotional intelligence.**

For our students, it starts with trust and relationship. Is the class well managed? Will I be safe here? Will people hurt or humiliate me? Will I be successful?

> **A CTS instructional system values "coverage" as its top priority. Pacing guides, district assessments, long lists of standards, curriculum maps, state testing, and teacher evaluation systems in sum convey a clear message: deliver the content.**

**Thoughtful teachers have long understood the importance of classroom culture.** Most highly successful teachers take the time to get to know their students, allow students to get to know them, build a predictable and secure classroom culture; develop classroom routines that help every student learn the behaviors that lead to success, practice these routines until they are consistently used by every student; and create opportunities for students to build relationships with each other. With a positive classroom culture in place, students are more likely to feel safe, be secure that in this place no one will hurt or embarrass them, stay engaged, be respectful of others, and make efforts to learn.

In a competency based learning system, we begin by identifying crucial outcomes. A thoughtfully considered system will include competencies in self-regulation, empathy, emotional intelligence, collaboration, problem-solving, and character. Academic content alone is not enough to prepare students for life.

In a competency based learning system, the development of the whole student will be considered, including academic learning, social-emotional learning, personal interests, and the habits of mind that are associated with long-term success in school and in life.

In a competency based learning system, students will clearly understand their learning goals and have models of what successful completion looks like. Teachers will adjust the pace and difficulty of instruction to match the student's readiness for every crucial learning outcome, so that each child has the opportunity to give effort and achieve success. Students will get the all the time needed for achievement of proficiency. No shortcuts will be taken which leave students with gaps in the development of crucial skills or concepts. Effort will be encouraged.

Students will consistently experience the connection between engagement and effort with successful learning. Motivation for learning will be enhanced by the experience of learning success within a safe learning environment. Students will own the desire to learn and the understanding that, with effort, they can always be a successful learner.

> **Any time, any place, any pace learning.**
>
> **Whole person learning.**
>
> **Learning that matters.**

# 11

# Creating the Culture of a Learning Organization

Imagine the daunting tasks in front of us.

**A university department** which has been accredited largely based on what gets covered within each degree program, and which for years has argued about the details of every course syllabus and curriculum plan, begins to move toward a competency based learning approach. Instead of measuring the number of credit hours in which a student has earned a "C" or better, the faculty begins to design a competency based structure in which each degree or certificate has a set of essential learning outcomes along with student directed learning outcomes. Not only that, but now students can use previous life experiences and out-of-school experiences to develop and demonstrate proficiency in these outcomes as part of their degree program. Without competency, students do not earn the degree. After demonstrating competency in every essential (content and/or skill) learning outcome along with additional student-directed learning goals, the student earns the degree or certificate.

The department goes to work, establishing a competency framework which matches present and future needs for skills and knowledge in each degree and certificate program. They clearly define each competency, and consider a process through which students can develop a plan to demonstrate each competency. Staff works collaboratively to develop a process that allows student individual learning goals to be part of each student's comprehensive instructional plan. Courses are revised to match the learning needs of students working within this model. Some courses are broken up into modules which can be used to match specific student learning needs.

Apprenticeships, internships, on-line learning options, and a host of other ways to learn are considered and cataloged as options to consider within the development of a plan that meets the needs of a student and also holds to a high standard for learning outcomes.

**A high school** begins to experiment with competency based programming. At first they take some easy steps. Participation in sports can be used to earn a required credit in Physical Education. A co-op or internship position can be used for credit if the responsibilities match up to the expectations for a math, business, or social studies course. On-line learning options outside of the school day are considered for credit and testing out opportunities for some required courses are made available. In these cases, the basic system of course and credit requirements has been maintained.

This high school staff and the school board decide to go further. They begin the process of looking at each course and considering what learning outcomes are essential for a student's graduation, and more importantly for success in life. The grading structure is called into question. No longer can you pass with a C. Students can complete a course as soon as they have demonstrated competency in all essential outcomes for a course. Students can also take a course as many times as needed to achieve competency in any of the identified essential outcomes.

A myriad of options and questions emerged. How will the school define clear criteria for competency so that all staff holds to the same standards? How do we include student and parent input into the design of a learning plan? At what point do we forget about credits and grades, and simply work toward the defined competencies we have established as a baseline for graduation?

Some students have gaps in understanding basic level (i.e. 2nd–3rd grade) math skills. Can the school structure learning opportunities which meet these and other similar learning needs?

What are the steps that lead to the development of graduation-level outcomes, and how do we help students develop absolute competency for each step along the path to those outcomes? Can we certify students in skills which go beyond the skills which are required for high school graduation? Can we collaborate with local businesses to build competency profiles which match the needs of local employers and keep jobs and companies in the community? How do we maintain an emphasis on developing a well-rounded student and maintain instruction designed to explore and extend knowledge?

**At a middle school,** recognizing the diverse learning needs among their students, educators decide to skip over the stage of aligning competencies with courses. They identify core middle school completion competencies and pathways to achieving these competencies. Included among their core competencies are social-emotional skills and self-regulatory skills. They develop data tracking systems to follow the progress of each student. Because so many of the crucial competencies overlap between disciplines, science and math instructors look for ways to work together. Project based and activity based learning is used to challenge students and allow them to work at the optimal level of challenge for each student. Collaboration is encouraged.

Home learning, summer learning, experience-based learning, blended learning, and other options are explored. Report cards are an analysis of progress toward the middle school core competencies.

**At a state department of education,** officials recognize the ridiculous nature of the Continuing Education Unit (CEU) system we've historically used for maintaining professional certificates. One CEU equals ten contact hours. If you are present, and remember to sign in and sign out, you earn your contact hours.

During training hours some teachers are playing on their phones. Others may be drifting off into out of body experiences. The learning needs of the educators are not assessed in this process. The quality of instruction is not considered. Learning outcomes are not considered. CEUs are all about seat time and have never equated to learning or to teaching skills.

The department of education begins the process of change. A careful review of the measurable skills needed for entry level and tenured teachers are considered. A framework for the steps to professional competency is established. The role of teacher training institutions, professional associations, and school districts for the basic, remedial, and advanced training needs of educators is discussed. The department decides that if we want the best teachers, we must have a plan for professional learning that leads to skills that matter.

**At an elementary school,** educators make a commitment to helping every child build a solid foundation of basic skills by the end of third grade, and then to refine these skills with an emphasis on intrinsic motivation to learn and personal habits of learning. These educators choose a competency based framework for all the domains of early childhood (i.e. *Essential Skills Inventory, Preschool through Grade 3*, Sornson, 2012), and they identify core upper elementary competencies which integrate with the middle school core competencies. Report cards are aligned with the competencies and serve as a way to deepen communication with parents regarding the developmental process and the development of the whole child.

With a long history of covering lessons and moving along with the pacing guide, teachers must relearn basic planning and instructional practices. The habit of teaching without regard for student readiness is hard to break. Teachers are challenged to be consistent as they collect high-quality observational data. Improved data leads to improved differentiated instruction, and teachers begin to collaborate more to share ideas about both embedded assessment and informed differentiated instruction. As they get to understand student learning needs better, especially in social-emotional, language development, and sensory-motor domains, staff find themselves more deeply understanding the connections between domains, and building better relationships with students.

**At a preschool,** the staff has always been tuned into the development of the whole child, but now begins to use a competency framework which helps them define crucial outcomes in each domain. Activity within a learning domain is not confused with competency. Teachers are able to recognize any gaps in development, and also when to accelerate instruction to meet the needs of each child.

Because preschool teachers are always busy, it can be challenging to develop the habits of systematically monitoring progress in each of the early childhood domains. For some teachers it is difficult to learn to embed assessment into the process of instruction; somehow assessment has been connected to one-on-one time away from instruction. But now the staff is learning to assess student learning while kids are engaged in the natural process of learning. For some it is hard to trust their own observations, and to assume that parents and administrators will give validity to the data which is based on their observations. Clear systems for on-going assessment must be developed and implemented.

Teachers learn to assess essential skills using several different learning situations, materials, and formats. Teachers learn that quality observational assessment, judgments based on careful scrutiny, using specific rubrics, over several days, using multiple learning situations is far more reliable than any snap-shot one day paper and pencil assessment. They learn to share strategies for both assessment and instruction with each other. Professional respect is enhanced, and collaboration becomes the norm rather than the exception.

## Creating a Learning Culture

One assumption used in each of the above descriptions is that adult educators have the capacity to work together and learn together in collaborative groups. For this to occur, competency based schools will need to work to create the conditions for high quality adult learning.

Like children, in fact like all humans, we learn better and collaborate better when we work within a culture of trust, safety, positive communication, and personal connection. But the top-down authoritarian design of Taylor and the historic use of separate classrooms for delivering instruction have not contributed to the development of collaborative cultures in our schools. In the same way that a thoughtful classroom teacher takes the time to develop a positive classroom culture, teacher leaders and administrative leaders look for ways to enhance connection, build trust, build awareness, create teams, grow human capacity, build habits of continuous learning, and learn to be collaborative learning teams. Creating the conditions for great learning and collaboration becomes a priority in a competency based learning environment.

> **For decades, state and district education officials have set the expectations for what should be taught, in what order, and at what age. In recent years politicians and bureaucrats have further dictated when and how this content will be tested, how schools will be graded, and how teachers will be evaluated. We are in the strong arms of a top-down Taylorian approach to every aspect of managing public education.**

## Changing Old Habits

Changing the habits of adults is a challenge. Often we are barely conscious of our routines; these are just the patterns of our days. But the routines of a top-down authoritarian Taylorian model for schools is not consistent with the routines needed for a collaborative learning environment moving toward effective competency based learning.

A competency based learning model challenges many of the standard practices of this authoritarian style. The CBL model assumes that teachers understand their students well enough to adjust the instructional plan, assumes that teachers work with students to determine learning interests and styles, and assumes that teachers work together to help each other grow expert in observational and systematic assessment as well as differentiated instruction to meet student learning needs. Teachers who are comfortable following a top-down instructional plan will have many new habits and skills to learn in the CBL school.

Educators will also be challenged to learn how to **balance coverage with competency** in a school which embraces competency based learning. A comprehensive plan for instruction will embrace exploration and enrichment, which might well include whole class learning and a curriculum plan for covering content at a grade or stage in student development. But in a CBL school **developing competency in essential skills will take priority over keeping up with the pacing guide.**

Learning for enrichment, exploration, and pure pleasure are crucial for a well-rounded education. In the CBL world, we will look for ways to embrace pathways to competency along with many opportunities to stretch awareness, stimulate curiosity, **and develop enthusiastic learners for life.** Teacher leaders, administrative leaders, and parents working together are challenged to create new models of instruction that will establish pathways to competency within a culture of scholarship.

As we move toward competency based learning systems we will need **clear exit standards** for graduation from high school, course completion, and certificate or university degree completion.

There may be differences between the desired exit outcomes in schools and communities based on culture, geography, or the needs of local employers. There may be differences among the exit outcomes developed by different institutions based on the expertise and interests of community leaders. Students and their families will face choices between institutions which have different visions for student learning.

We will need **clear standards for competency at every step along the pathway** to our long-term learning outcomes.

Once exit outcomes are established, it will be our responsibility to establish a framework of competencies which allows students to fully develop the skills and knowledge which leads to the exit outcomes.

If you are an educator during the advent of competency based learning, opportunities for learning and collaboration await. For most schools and districts, creating the conditions for safe and collaborative adult learning and identifying key learning skills or outcomes for all staff will be among the first steps toward competency based learning.

# 12

# Learning for Understanding and Application

I remember learning to sail on Lake Charlevoix in northern Michigan. For years I'd watched the beautiful boats tighten their sails and lean into the wind, come about and elegantly shift direction, or fly downwind with mainsail and spinnaker out wide and full. In my small sailboat I practiced tightening my sails and heading as close into the wind as possible, changing tack and moving across the direction of the wind, shifting the rudder and releasing the sail at just the right moment so that I could catch the wind and gracefully find my new tack.

At first it was not so graceful. When changing direction, the boom might crack my head when I forgot to duck at the right moment. Sometimes my timing was poor, and I failed to build up enough speed to complete the change of direction, and my sails would flap helplessly as the wind tossed me about. But occasionally I would get it right.

"Coming about," I'd yell, even if I was all alone in the small boat. Build up the speed, shift the rudder hard, release the sail, duck, hold the rudder, catch the sail on the other side of the mast, and bind the line. Then the wind would fill the sails and the mast would arch, and the boat would catch its speed and shoot forward in a new direction. I'd sail for hours, loving every turn, every long run into the wind, every failure, and every moment of grace.

Learning is joyful. As humans, with our oversized cerebral and prefrontal cortex, we are wired to learn. When we have learning goals that are clear, attainable, and personally meaningful, a gang of thugs could not deter our desire to learn.

> **Competency based learning is focused on student learning outcomes, and is built with the following design principles in mind:**
>
> ♦ **Students advance upon mastery, not age.**
> ♦ **The pathway to competency is built with explicit and measurable learning objectives.**
> ♦ **Assessment is primarily formative, and skills or concepts are assessed in multiple contexts to guarantee both deep understanding and application.**

A child watches in wonder as her parent reads a story. Her mom can decipher the squiggly symbols on a page, use her voice to convey excitement or danger, sadness or love, and make characters come alive. At some point the child learns that this magic we call reading can be hers. Step by step, adults help her learn to read. "What's this word?" "Now try to read the whole sentence." At every step, the goals are clear. At every step, the goals are attainable. This child believes she can learn to read. She wants to read, and she wants to practice reading.

In a musical family, a child is given a guitar. For years, other members of the family have made instruments come alive, and now it's his turn, his instrument, his desire. Every new chord is a victory. Every new song is a celebration. Every day he finds time to practice. Every day he is a step closer to his goal.

An adolescent is focused on her video game. The graphics are great and the content intriguing. She is at level three, and so close to level four. If she could only kill a few more gorgons, or remember to get help from the lady with the light saber who is hiding in the second cave after the river crossing. For hours, she sits absorbed in her game. She never meant to spend all day indoors, but she is so close to getting to the next level.

In her Kindergarten class a student is learning to subitize, **which means quickly recognize the number value of a group.** Not all of the kids can do it. In the math center she works in a small group with her teacher, who shows her one side of the domino and points to a group of dots. "Six," she correctly identifies. They play with dice and dominoes for a few minutes, and this students almost always gets the answer quickly, without having to slow down and count each dot. The next day the teacher brings out an abacus at the math center, and moves a group of beads on the top row. "How many?" she asks and every time a student gets it right there are smiles. The next day the teacher has paper plates on which she has drawn sets of objects from two to ten. Every day it is something new. She learns to recognize the value of a group of buttons, beads, or checkers, or a value on the abacus, or a group of bean bags on the floor, or the number of chairs at a large table. Every day she looks forward to going to the math center. The teacher has a wonderful way of making it challenging but never so hard that it seems impossible.

On weekends a third grade student watches baseball with his Dad. It is a special time. They cheer, they root for their team, and after the game they go outside and play catch. This child dreams of being a ball player. During the week he keeps a ball and glove in his backpack just in case there might be someone who wants to play catch. At home during the week he practices throwing the ball on the garage roof, and catching it as it comes flying over the gutters. He's learned to catch almost anything which is thrown his way, on the ground or in the air. He can't wait for the spring baseball leagues to begin.

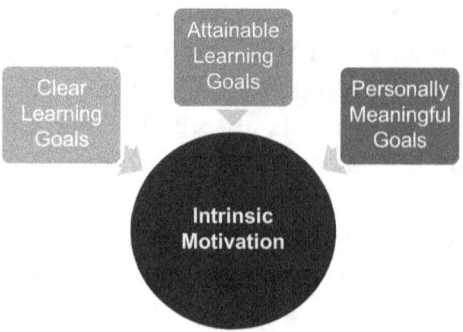

**FIGURE 12.1** Intrinsic Motivation

**Unfortunately the examples above contrast with most learning experiences in a typical Cover Test Sort school.** *Read* Chapter 9 *and answer the multiple choice questions at the end.* The learning goals of this assignment are entirely unclear. For some students the content of the chapter or the reading level may be too difficult, and this makes learning success unattainable. For other students the content may already be familiar, and nothing new is learned. In almost all cases, this kind of assignment is not personally meaningful, and is presented as something you must do and for which you will be punished with lousy grades if you answer the questions poorly.

*Finish this Word Search worksheet before the end of the class, and if you don't get it done, take it as homework.* If there are any imaginable learning goals for this assignment, they are unclear to most of us. For some this activity is drudgery, but possible. For others the activity is both difficult and drudgery. Only creatures from the Talarian Republic find this activity personally meaningful.

*There are two weeks left in the semester, and three more chapters to cover. Get ready, here it comes.* Whenever teaching and learning becomes a race, deep understanding suffers. Whenever the learning goals are to memorize a bunch of content to pass a test, the essence of learning has been perverted. After years of extrinsic direction to learn content which has little personal meaning, often boring, occasionally impossible, many students experience a diminution of intrinsic motivation to learn. Young children are naturally drawn to learning in every aspect of life, but after enough years of CTS, this love of learning can be lost.

**Consider the benefits of a well-designed competency based learning system** in which students work toward learning goals which are clear, attainable, and personally meaningful. Motivated and confident children are far more likely to develop the skills and habits that allow them to love learning for life.

## Clear Learning Goals

When students have a clear goal for learning, they are more able to stay focused on giving effort to achieve this outcome. *I want to be a good reader like Mom. I want to be able to quickly recognize the number groups. I want to catch every ball Dad throws to me.*

*Finish the chapter* is not a learning goal. *Try to do better* is not a clear goal. *Get a better grade* is a compliance goal, not a learning goal. *Bring treats to class for extra credit* has nothing to do with authentic learning outcomes. When students can clearly understand and visualize learning goals, they become real. They become attainable. It is possible to contrast the skills you have today with the outcomes you want, and be motivated to engage in a learning plan that helps you reach your goal.

Competency based learning pathways will have long-term goals (skills, knowledge, units, graduation, certification, or employment eligibility) with clear step by step increments of learning and skill that lead to these goals. Some students may wish to travel farther down a particular learning pathway than others, but every student will know where she is and where she wants to be in every crucial aspect of development. The clear understanding of each learning step along the pathway to an end goal vastly increases personal ownership of the learning task and motivation to learn.

## Attainable Learning Goals

When students believe that an outcome is possible for them, within their grasp, available to them with reasonable effort, they try harder. **All the research on instructional match,** instructional zone, and zone of proximal development makes it clear that students are more motivated, spend more time on task, and behave better when the learning task is just **a bit challenging without pushing them into the frustration zone** (Burns, 2007; Fuchs & Fuchs, 1988; Gickling & Armstrong, 1978; Vygotsky, 1978; Betts, 1946).

## Time in the Learning Frustration Zone Pushes Kids into Disengagement. Patterns of Disengagement can Impact Children for the Rest of their Lives.

When a child with a third grade reading level is given reading material at the fifth grade level, frustration is not far away. Rigid learning programs put many students at risk for the simple reason that they are not all at the same level of readiness.

> **The importance of allowing students to learn at the appropriate instructional level is one of the most well established points in all the literature on teaching and learning. Yet curriculum driven instruction trumps instructional match in CTS classrooms and schools across the nation and around the world.**

Every time a student says (or thinks), "I'm not good at math," it is likely an expression of poor learning experiences based on a curriculum-driven learning model. A few months or a few years of working unsuccessfully to keep up with the pace of instruction is enough for most kids to give up on a subject matter, or in some cases to give up on themselves.

In a typical classroom there are often some other students in class who lack motivation to learn for a very different reason. **They are bored.** They already know the skill or subject matter, and going through the lessons and practice sheets is an exercise in compliance to an uncaring authority. For these students the learning goals are not in the zone or proximal development because they have already been attained. Gaming designers understand this, and create higher levels of challenge within the structure of their product. Rigidly paced learning programs in school have not yet responded to this obvious need.

Students are far more motivated to learn when the task is a little bit challenging, but not overwhelming and frustrating.

**In a competency based learning system the steps along the pathway are clearly delineated.** Once competency is attained for a crucial skill, educators look for ways to move the student on to the next skill along the pathway. Keeping students at their instructional level can only be achieved by knowing your students well through ongoing formative assessment, and moving them at the right time along a clear pathway of skills leading to important long-term learning goals.

## Personally Meaningful Goals

Making learning goals clear and attainable significantly increases motivation and its byproducts, including time on task, attention, and rates of learning. But when you help students understand why a learning goal in important in their personal lives, and when you offer some opportunity to choose the skills or content which will be included in their learning program, motivation soars (Ames, 1992; Csikszentmihalyi, 1985; Driscoll, 1994; Lepper and Hodel, 1989; Mayer, 2002; Stiggins, 1999).

With young children it is often as simple as letting them pick an activity center or a book. As students get older, allowing them to participate in the planning of their learning process makes it more likely that you will see great effort and positive outcomes. Projects and activities which support progress along a competency pathway can easily be personalized.

By middle and high school students are capable of making choices regarding which content and/or skills they want to develop to a proficient level, and for which content/skills they would like to excel and go beyond typical standards for competency. Post high school learning should certainly include student planning input, with the end goal of competency within a personally designed learning plan.

> **We can never attain first-rate learning outcomes with a ram-it-down-their-throats approach to teaching students. Competency based learning gives us an opportunity to create a system that offers clear, attainable, and personally meaningful learning goals. By nurturing the intrinsic desire to learn and the joy of learning, we can help more of our students become successful learners for life.**

For students to take ownership of their own learning, observant parents and teachers watch carefully to see what special interest a child demonstrates. They allow time for exploration, play, and discovery before dumping too much content over the intrinsic fires of learning. Sometimes great teachers occasionally step back, watch and listen, perceive the direction in which student interest is developing, and then provide challenges and opportunities to further excite the desire to learn.

As we develop competency based learning systems, we will be challenged to ensure that we take advantage of the motivational power of clear, attainable, and personally meaningful learning goals. If students clearly understand the learning goal, see it as attainable, and appreciate the value it has to their personal lives, they will be far more motivated to learn. This motivation to learn directly improves outcomes and has the additional benefit of helping students discover how to become learners for life.

**Learning systems which give students a chance to move at their own pace from competency to competency will enhance intrinsic motivation.** They will help students see the connection between effort and the rewards of learning. And they could create generations of learners who understand that meaningful learning is possible any time, any place, and at any pace.

# 13

# Masters of the Trade: Game Designers

The designers of video games have applied the principles of competency based learning, in combination with other fundamental learning concepts, arguably better than anyone. You might question the content that some game creators use or the purposefulness of the activities, but you cannot question the efficacy of their design principles to interest gamers, hold attention, make it fun, and motivate players to want to come back for more. Consider these learning concepts and principles which are clearly demonstrated in high quality digital games.

## Students Advance Upon Mastery, not Age

Games have levels of challenge, and start with the acquisition of basic skills which are needed for success throughout the game. Models of success, video examples, or prompts are used to help gamers find success at the earliest levels. Players are never pushed to a higher level based on age, time given to the task, or any other reason until they are capable of success at the next level.

## Tiered Learning

Vygotsky would be proud of the care with which designers craft tiers of learning. With every new level, the knowledge and skills picked up in previous levels can be applied to help the gamer be successful. Sometimes a skill or idea is introduced at one level, and then opportunities to use or practice that skill become available after several more steps have been mastered. At lower levels, players are taught to use skills within a simple context. As they progress through the levels, the skill is used within a more complex situation, or used in combination with other skills.

## Instructional Zone

Success breeds success, unless it comes too easily. Designers artfully apply the research on instructional match, instructional zone, and zone of proximal development. The player is challenged enough so that she never gets bored. She is highly engaged and motivated by the challenge. The player is also never challenged to the point that she disengages and wants to quit. Designers write exquisite algorithms to balance the need for a high degree of success and just enough challenge.

## Trial and Error

The games encourage players to try something, see if it works, reflect, form a hypothesis, visualize an action plan, try something new, and repeat the process. Within a carefully designed plan for each player to be successful, reaching your goals can only occur through action. Players learn to try stuff and see what works. This feedback loop is quick and consistent.

## Explicit Learning Objectives

The pathway to success is built with explicit objectives. Players know what they are trying to achieve. They are glad to give effort to achieve this clear objective, and are happy to learn from the experiences of others. With explicit goals, gamers become problem-solvers, using previously acquired knowledge along with skills and tactics.

## Motivation to take on Challenges

Successful video games are difficult. Gamers want to take on challenges, solve problems, collaborate, and persist. Gamers intrinsically want to learn more skills and get better at the game. Contrast that with students in many classrooms who want to do as little as possible to get a good grade, as judged by someone else, when working on obscure and personally meaningless learning objectives.

## Embedded Assessment

Game designers do not use end of unit assessments and they don't give grades. There is no Bell Curve. Instead, assessment is embedded into every moment of the game. The level of difficulty is increased only when the student is ready for the challenge, as demonstrated by her level of play. Every moment of play is used as part of the formative assessment process to determine whether to present new challenges or take the player to the next level.

## Identity and Networks of Support

Gamers see themselves as learning and getting better, with the end goal of beating the game or an opponent. They often form support networks with friends or colleagues who share tactics, experiences, and suggestions for improvement. With every new skill, with every new level, with every victory their identity as a learner is reinforced.

Competency based learning systems have the potential to take learning to a whole new level for our society. When combined with good learning principles, and a little common sense, we can design learning systems at school, at home, and in our communities which bring learning to life for generations of children and adults. While video game designers want to sell games and keep gamers engaged, they nonetheless have applied the research on motivation and learning far better than most school district instructional leaders.

# 14

# What's Happening in Competency Based Learning Initiatives

Even during the Covid-19 pandemic years of 2020 to 2022, **most schools held onto the curriculum-driven system of covering mandated content.** On-line versions of content coverage lessons and units were made virtually available to students during the enforced time away from school. In most schools, after missing months or in some cases years of in-person instruction, students came back to the next grade and began working on the next grade's content expectations, **whether they were ready or not.**

But change starts slowly. Many students experienced diminished learning or learning losses during their absence from school, and in some schools and states, questions about the efficacy of the existing instructional model grew louder.

In an article in the Washington Post, Nancy Walser (August 13, 2021) reported, "Once considered a boutique form of education overly reliant on technology, competency-based education is increasingly seen as a way to solve a host of problems with traditional schooling, problems that became more apparent when learning went virtual. Traditional school metrics—based on attendance ("seat time") and meeting a minimal standard to move to the next grade—often lead to arbitrary grading practices, uninspiring lessons and a lack of flexibility to support students socially and emotionally, critics say. They argue that challenging students to demonstrate competency on critical concepts only after they are prepared is a better and more motivating way to measure learning, and allows educators to address gaps before they grow over time."

Competency based learning is slowly moving into the mainstream of thought, if not yet practice. In the post article several leaders in emerging practice were interviewed. Jean-Claude Brizard, president and CEO of Digital Promise, said, "There is real appetite for something more whole-child, more comprehensive, more longitudinal, that really informs [teacher] practice," he said, adding, "Competency-based assessment does a much better job, frankly, of really informing practice."

Lillian Pace, the vice-president of policy and advocacy for KnowledgeWorks, stated, "Pre-pandemic, we saw a lot more interest in one-off pilot programs. The pandemic really changed the policy conversation to more systemic shifts" (Walser, 2021).

The status quo persists, but there are a growing number of successful competency based learning initiatives that have taken root around the country and around the world.

## State Competency Based Learning Initiatives

A large majority of states have some provision in state regulations which allows school districts to opt out of traditional Carnegie unit seat time requirements for graduation.

Alabama policy states that "one credit may be granted in Grade 9–12 for required or elective course consisting of a minimum of 140 instructional hours **or** in which students demonstrate mastery of Alabama course of study content standards in one-credit courses without specified instructional time." Kentucky allows schools to award competency based credits if they have developed specific criteria for determining proficiency. Oregon was among the first states to enable districts to develop proficiency systems for the awarding of credit, and has supported the development of competency based learning pilot sites. Iowa allows both competency based and time-based credits for graduation. Ohio allows credit flexibility based on a state-approved waiver system, and permits districts to include distance learning, after school programming, internships, and community service as part of their pathways to competency.

Since 2005, New Hampshire has taken a leadership position in the development of competency based learning systems. The state legislature approved the *Minimum Standards for Public School Approval*, under which districts were required to create standards for competency and begin measuring course credit in these terms by the start of the 2009–10 school year. This was the first statewide effort to create a competency based learning system, and the minimum standards have been subsequently updated (New Hampshire DOE, 2014).

Local districts were given broad discretion in the interpretation and implementation of the New Hampshire competency mandate. Some districts became quickly invested in the opportunity to build flexible, personalized programming while others have stayed with more familiar curriculum-driven methodologies. But state leadership in New Hampshire has persisted toward a different learning model. A guide for districts, *New Hampshire's Vision for Redesign, Moving from High Schools to Learning Communities*, was approved (New Hampshire DOE, 2007). New teacher training regulations were approved in 2011, and administrative rules were updated in 2014 to further support the transition toward competency based learning. A collection of resources developed by New Hampshire educators to support extended learning opportunities are available at **beyondclassroom.org.**

One of the factors motivating change in New Hampshire is the desire to reduce the incidence of high school dropouts. In addition to the state mandate to create more personalized competency based learning options, the age at which a student could drop out of school was raised to 18. In 2002, 25% of high school students dropped out before graduation. By 2011 the rate was 4.68% and falling.

Maine also developed a strategic plan for learner-centered instruction, *Education Evolving: Maine's Plan for Putting Learners First* (Maine DOE, 2012). The core priorities of the plan include:

- Effective, Learner-Centered Instruction.
- Great Teachers and Leaders.
- Multiple Pathways for Learner Achievement.
- Comprehensive School and Community Supports.
- Coordinated and Effective State Support.

According to the plan, students in Maine would demonstrate proficiency in eight subjects, including English, math, science, social studies, and health/physical education for graduation. With grant support from the Nellie Mae Foundation, two of Maine's largest districts, Portland and Sanford, began to work toward the transformation to a personalized competency based graduation system. **But implementation efforts across the state ran into questions and challenges they could not resolve, and the effort was abandoned.** The Maine experience serves as a cautionary tale regarding the importance of having a vigorous plan to support quality implementation of this new model for learning.

Vermont requires districts to establish standards of proficiency for graduation, to use tiered systems of support to assist all students working toward the standards, and to develop personalized learning plans for students in grades 7 to 12. Vermont began issuing proficiency based diplomas in 2020.

> "Proficiency-based learning" and "proficiency-based graduation" refers to systems of instruction, assessment, grading and academic reporting that are based on students demonstrating mastery of the knowledge and skills they are expected to learn before they progress to the next lesson, get promoted to the next grade level, or receive a diploma.
>
> – Vermont Education Quality Standards, 2013

Colorado has approved a multi-year process of developing and implementing state guidelines for graduation requirements. Starting with 9th graders in 2017–18, and with full implementation by 2020–21, these guidelines will include new academic standards and individual career and academic plans for each student. Local school districts will be able to select options by which their students can demonstrate competency, with options to include coursework, minimum scores on state or national tests, rigorous learning projects, college level courses, and professional certificates. Colorado predicts that by 2020, 74% of jobs in Colorado will require education beyond high school (Colorado Dept. of Education, 2013).

In Illinois a group of districts formed a competency based high school graduation pilot program. Arizona developed an option for high school students to earn a proficiency based diploma. Dozens of states have developed study committees or grants to support CBL pilot projects.

The Council of Chief State School Officers (CCSSO) has developed the Innovation Lab Network (ILN) to share learning, drive collective action, and to create and scale student-centered learningenvironments. In their publication, *Innovation in Action: State Pathways for Advancing StudentCentered Learning* (CCSSO, 2013), they call for states to:

- Define and systematize college and career readiness consistent with deeper learning.
- Enable personalized learning and prepare the educator workforce so that all students can succeed.
- Establish balanced systems of assessment to meaningfully measure college and career readiness.
- Anchor accountability in college and career readiness.
- Develop seamless pathways to college and career.

The development and use of competency based learning, while not a new idea, presents many opportunities for innovation. States can serve as incubators for that innovation, and hopefully we can all reap the bounty of the best ideas that are emerging in every corner of the nation.

Innovation is the creation and development of new ideas.

- Which states will abandon the Carnegie unit and course credit requirement system for high school altogether, and replace it with a clearly defined set of outcome competencies?
- Will some states move to a competency certificate program, specifically describing the knowledge and skills students have developed to proficiency?
- Might states choose differing sets of outcomes as crucial to life readiness based on their assessment of the needs of their citizens and workforce in the future?
- Who will develop explicit pathways to their college and career readiness standards, and use technology systems to help track individual progress?
- Which states will recognize the importance of competency based learning systems and develop statewide systems to help more children build crucial foundation skills during the early childhood years?

## Competency Based Learning in Post-secondary Education

Post-secondary education has responded more vigorously to the opportunities presented by competency based learning than any other segment of the education system. Colleges, universities, community colleges, technical schools, and certification programs compete for students are becoming responsive to the needs of adult learners who come to higher education knowing different things, needing different outcomes, and learning at different rates and in different ways.

These schools/organizations are also responding to poor program completion rates and the concern that many college degrees are irrelevant to the needs of the workplace. They are finding ways to use the availability of technology for instruction, assessment, and personalization of learning. While medical and vocational/technical training programs have long included a competency based component, the application of competency to other degree and certificate programs is quickly developing.

In the 1970s, competency based learning programs at institutes for higher learning began to emerge, in part because of a concern for the growing number of adults returning to college. Colleges began to develop prior learning assessments (PLA) to acknowledge learning from other institutions, from military training, or other sources. Generally, these competencies were then translated into course-based college credits. Innovative college programs emerged at Empire State College, Regents College, Thomas Edison State College, Alverno College, DePaul University's School for New Learning, and other institutions.

With the advent of on-line learning, Institutions of Higher Education (IHEs) began to grapple with the uncomfortable problem of assigning credit for learning that did not take place in the classroom, and therefore could not be measured in class hours per week. **No one could know exactly how much time an on-line student spent on a learning module or test. As measurement of time became less reliable, measurement of learning became more important.**

Measurement of learning continues to increase in importance. The need for more adults to access relevant skill-based post-secondary training, the availability of free Massive Open Online Courses (MOOCs), the quality and availability of digital learning programs, and the desire for more personalized learning programs have made universities and other learning institutions increasingly offer competency based learning options for their students.

**Every month in seems more options become available.** Some institutions use competency frameworks within a course-based system. This approach may include testing out, assignment of credit for previous life experiences, blended learning, and/or the completion of online modules to earn course credit. This maintains the familiar credit structure found in most colleges and universities.

Other institutions have stepped away from the credit/course model. They start by establishing clear competency exit outcomes for a degree or certificate and assessing the student's level of knowledge and skill in relation to these outcomes. Additional learning goals based on student interest are considered. A learning program is designed to match the needs of each student which could include courses, MOOCs, internships, projects, independent study, or other experiences. A coach or mentor works with the student to facilitate learning and assess progress. Cohort groups may be used to further support learning. And only when the student has demonstrated competency in each essential program outcome is the degree or certificate awarded.

Western Governors University was chartered in 1996, supported by the Western Governors Association, to use competencies rather than seat time as the measure of its outcomes, and to take advantage of distance learning opportunities. It has grown to become an accredited national university, with more than 50,000 students in all 50 states, offering competency based degrees at the associate, bachelor, and master's levels. WGU's on-line programs use tests, projects, papers, and practical demonstrations of a required skill to demonstrate mastery, and allow students to advance upon competency rather than using time limited course options. At WGU there are no required courses, just required competencies. Working with a faculty advisor, students work out a personalized plan for reaching the competencies required in a program, and are charged a flat fee per term rather than by credit hours.

At DePaul University's School for New Learning (SNL), students earn degrees by demonstrating the competencies required for the degree. They can take courses that are related to those competencies or develop portfolios that demonstrate mastery of those competencies through prior learning. Some coursework is required.

Excelsior College School of Nursing has offered an accredited competency based associates degree for almost four decades. The program is designed for students transitioning from a Licensed Practical Nurse to a Registered Nurse role, or coming to nursing with a clinical background. Students complete general education requirements through coursework, must successfully demonstrate nursing clinical skills, and pass a computer simulation examination measuring clinical competence.

The University of Maine at Presque Isle has begun a multi-year process to base all of its academic programs on "proficiencies" that students must master to earn a degree. Students will progress through in-person, online, and hybrid degree programs by demonstrating proficiency in required concepts. Northern Arizona University students pay a flat fee for a six-month "subscription" to classes at NAU. During that time they are free to take—and earn credit for—as many on-line courses as possible, within three available undergraduate degree programs.

Capella University has mapped academic and professional standards to all degree programs, and its **FlexPath allows students to complete as many courses per quarter as they can** for one flat tuition rate in the departments of business, information technology, and psychology. Davenport University offers an online self-paced competency based MBA.

Even large public universities have made the move toward competency based learning. The University of Wisconsin offers its Flexible Option, comprised of five competency-based online programs leading to a certificate or bachelor's degree. Purdue University offers a transdisciplinary bachelor's degree program based on learned and demonstrated competencies at the Purdue Polytechnic Institute and the College of Technology.

The University of Michigan has established a master's degree program for health profession educators, partly in response to a national shortage of medical school faculty. The MHPE program prepares practicing professionals in medicine, nursing, dentistry, pharmacy, public health, social work, and other health professions to become health profession educators. This competency based degree is not based on credit hour requirements.

MPHE students choose from among 21 competencies, which are tied to various health professions. Each enrolling student's experience and previous learning is reviewed by a competency assessment panel, and then assigned credit for existing competencies. Students are assigned a mentor, and an individualize program is designed to meet the needs of each student. The pace of the program is flexible. For the degree, students must provide documentation and evidence of competency, which could be a paper, video presentation, PowerPoint, grant application, portfolio or some combination of multiple pieces of evidence, and pass a final summative assessment based on their learning portfolio.

Interest in higher education CBE continues to pick up steam. In July 2014, the U.S. House passed H.R. 3136, the **Advancing Competency-Based Education Demonstration Project Act.** The vote was unanimous, 414-0.

Competency based learning has emerged as a viable model for post-secondary education. But as each new CBE program is developed there are questions. How do we define specific required competencies? Are some competencies more important than others? Can there be different levels of competency? Can a student add personally meaningful competencies to a degree or certificate plan? Are there multiple pathways to a given competency? What are the acceptable demonstrations of competency? Do our proofs/demonstrations accurately describe the ability to understand a body of knowledge, develop a skill, or apply this skill? How do we train faculty to use consistent and effective assessment protocols? How do we train faculty to be skilled at differentiation of the learning experience? What is the role of credit or grades, and how can these be transferred from one institution to another? As competency based learning blends with and in some cases replaces curriculum-driven methodologies, how do we ensure quality?

> **The issue of quality among competency based learning systems is pressing. Some institutions of higher education, in the race to find more students or sell more credits, might choose a less demanding road to CBE. For those institutions considering a move to competency based learning, consider this rubric for quality CBE.**

# A Rubric for Considering the Quality of Higher Education Competency Based Learning Initiatives

**Level 1**

- A set of knowledge competencies has been established for each course.
- Students work to achieve these competencies by the end of semester/year.
- Students who do not achieve every competency will repeat the course.

**Level 2**

- A set of knowledge competencies has been established for each course.
- Students can test out of courses in which they have expertise and experience.
- Students can move through course modules or chapters at their own pace.
- Passing chapter/module tests and completion of other required assignments (papers, journals, etc.) is considered completion of course credit and/or competency.
- Community service, internships, observation, performance groups, or similar experiences will be considered as the equivalent to a required course or competency.

**Level 3**

- Competencies for each required course are clearly established, including knowledge, skill, and application.
- Students are assessed to determine existing knowledge/skill/application levels, and can test out of a course by demonstrating knowledge, skill, and application.
- Students have personalized learning plans focused on achieving the required learning objectives at their own pace.

- Learning plans can include specific modules, learning materials, or experiences.
- Students receive frequent and systematic assessment of progress.
- Timely support is available.
- Students advance upon demonstrated mastery of learning goals leading to required competencies.

**Level 4**

- Minimum competencies are established for a certificate or degree including knowledge, skill, and application.
- A review/assessment of knowledge, skill, and application helps determine each student's learning needs within the program.
- Personalized learning plans focus on achievement of the required competencies.
- Specific short-term learning plans are developed by the facilitator and student, and can include specific modules, learning materials, or experiences.
- Students receive frequent and systematic assessment of progress.
- Timely support is available.
- Students advance upon demonstrated mastery of learning goals leading to required competencies.
- Degree or certificate is awarded upon demonstration of all required competencies.

**Level 5**

- Minimum competencies are established for a certificate or degree including knowledge, skill, and application.
- Additional learning goals are established based on the individual needs and interests of the student.
- A review/assessment of knowledge, skill, and application helps determine each student's learning needs within the program.

- A review/assessment of the student's learning strengths and style helps contribute to the development of a personalized learning plan.
- Personalized learning plans focus on achievement of the required competencies and the student's chosen goals.
- Specific short-term learning plans are developed by the facilitator and student, and can include specific modules, learning materials, or experiences.
- Cohort groups, on-line networks, or other support group structures are available.
- Students receive frequent and systematic assessment of progress.
- Timely instructional support is available.
- Students advance upon demonstrated mastery of learning goals leading to required competencies and student-initiated learning goals.
- Degree or certificate is awarded upon demonstration of all required competencies.

As competency based learning continues to expand within post-secondary education, professional organizations are stepping up to provide leadership and establish standards of practice. The American Association of Colleges and Universities (AAC&U) developed the Liberal Education and America's Promise (LEAP) initiative, which champions the importance of a 21st-century liberal education. LEAP has identified "Essential Learning Outcomes", covering broad knowledge areas, cognitive and practical skills, and the application of knowledge and skill to complex problems.

The Lumina Foundation developed the Degree Qualifications Profile (DQP) to provide a baseline set of reference points for what students should know and be able to do to earn an associate's, bachelor's, and master's degree. The DQP defines educational outcomes in terms of what graduates know and can do in the areas of applied learning, intellectual skills, specialized knowledge, broad knowledge, and civic learning.

The Western Association of Schools and Colleges, the Higher Learning Commission, the Southern Association of

Colleges and Schools, the Council of Independent Colleges and Universities, and several universities are working with the Lumina Foundation to test and further develop the DQP.

The Association of American Colleges and Universities is developing a competency based framework for undergraduate education called General Education Maps and Markers (GEMs), to align with the Degree Qualifications Profile (DQP).

The Global Learning Qualifications Profile (GLQP) was developed by Open SUNY, based in part on the LEAP project's essential learning outcomes and rubrics. The GLQP emphasizes assessment of college-level outcomes obtained through open learning sources including Open Educational Resources (OERs), Massive Open Online Courses (MOOCs), and prior or experiential learning.

The National Association of Manufacturers' Manufacturing Skills Certification System has developed a structure of stackable credentials indicating that workers have attained competencies for increasingly sophisticated levels of work across many areas of manufacturing, from machine operator to engineer to management positions. The essential elements of the Skills Certification System are:

- A collection of competencies that together defines a successful, high-performance manufacturing workforce.
- Industry-driven certifications that align with competencies.
- Best-in-class curriculum to articulate into for-credit education pathways that will ensure students achieve the competencies necessary to achieve industry credentials.

**Post-secondary education has discovered competency based learning and the process of experimentation and innovation has begun.**

The limitations of a time-bound learning system are starting to be widely recognized among the public and institutions of higher learning (Laitinen, 2012). When many university graduates cannot find professional jobs, and when growing businesses can't find new employees with the skills needed for success on the job, a new model begins to emerge. There are tens of millions of adults of all ages who need to complete a degree, earn a certificate, or update skills to match the changing job requirements of the information and technology society, for whom a competency based learning system just makes sense.

As we step free of the time-bound system we must create a competency based system that truly measures learning, that is clear in describing its learning objectives and transparent in its practice of measuring progress toward competency. Higher education is asked to do so many things, from offering training for specific technical skills to nurturing poets and artists, from developing well-rounded leaders to training scientists and researchers with eclectic interests and specific knowledge and skills. As the need for better, faster, and more flexible pathways to modern job skills continues to push us toward competency based learning, we are challenged to find the balance between liberal education, civic and character education, and technical learning. We are at the dawn of the age of personalized, flexible, lifelong learning.

## Competency Based Learning in Secondary Schools

Much of the attention given to competency based learning has been at the secondary level and focused on reaching standards for high school graduation. The conventional pattern of required classes and credits for high school graduation presents a litany of obvious questions.

- ♦ Why can't participation in sports take the place of a required PE credit?
- ♦ Can a student who takes advanced math from Kumon or Khan Academy be given credit?
- ♦ Why do we push some kids through the curriculum when we know they are not ready?

- Why do we require that other kids take classes in which they are already proficient?
- Do all students learn best with 180 days of instruction?
- Why exactly do we take summers off?

In recent years many of the questions have been related to economic and social concerns. Does graduation from high school mean anything? Are graduates ready for employment? Are they ready for college? Does a diploma indicate that basic math and ready skills are in place? Are graduating students prepared to be lifelong learners? What does graduation mean? Does our system stack the deck against poor children?

**Nations around the world** have recognized the need to improve education outcomes in response to new social, economic, and technical realities. The European Union has identified key competencies in its *European Framework of Key Competences for Lifelong Learning* (European Commission, 2007). This framework defines eight key competences and describes the essential knowledge, skills, and attitudes related to each of these. These key competences are: communication in the mother tongue, communication in foreign languages, math competence and basic competences in science and technology, digital competence, learning to learn, social and civic competencies, sense of initiative and entrepreneurship, and cultural awareness and expression. Each of the 28 European Union nations is approaching competency based learning in its own way.

Finland's approach includes a systemic approach to individualization of learning in the tenth through twelfth grades. Students build their personalized learning schedule made up of 70 minute classes, six week units, and the opportunity to progress at their own pace.

In Sweden, a group of 33 Kunskapsskolan (knowledge schools) operates with personalized learning pathways in which students track their own learning progress, beginning in eighth grade. Three levels of student mastery of competencies along the learning pathways is available, to be chosen with the advice of a personal coach.

In British Columbia a strong initiative supporting personalized learning and the development of competency is described in the *British Columbia Education Plan* (BC Ministry of Education, 2015), and detailed in *Exploring Curriculum Design, Transforming Curriculum and Assessment* (BC Ministry of Education, 2013). Alberta's development plan for competency based learning is described in *Framework for Student Learning: Competencies for Engaged Thinkers and Ethical Citizens with an Entrepreneurial Spirit* (Alberta Education, 2011).

Competency based learning is the recognized training method for vocational education and training (VET) in Australia. National standards define general competencies in the workplace, and specific units of competency can be set for an industry or a specific enterprise. In most Australian states, students can access this training at age 16, with more than half of all VET students over the age of 25.

**In the United States,** with permissive language allowing competency based alternatives to Carnegie units based on seat time available in most states, new models of competency based learning are emerging. Changing from a curriculum-driven to a competency based model is challenging, much like redesigning an airplane while it's still flying through the air. **A small but growing group of leaders in local school districts and schools across the nation have stepped up to the task.**

In New Hampshire, with its strong state-level competency initiative, districts have embraced competency to different degrees. In some schools required high school classes are aligned with competencies and graduation is based on competency, but students are not yet able to move at a flexible or individualized pace. Some schools have used technology or digital learning to complement traditional classroom instruction. Other schools have more vigorously pursued options including testing out, extended learning opportunities outside of the traditional classroom (apprenticeships, community service, independent study, internships, performing groups, private instruction), project-based learning, authentic assessment, portfolios, blended and/or digital learning.

**New Hampshire schools are adopting competency based learning in varied ways.**

Almost a quarter of the 250+ students at **Pittsfield Middle-High School** spend part of the school day, after-school hours, or summertime earning credits through activities outside regular classes, such as assisting dentists, accompanying midwives, designing websites, volunteering in kindergarten classrooms, or working at local newspapers. They earn both core and elective credits for such activities, produce a portfolio of work, and offer presentations to show they've developed competencies.

Teachers at **Newfound Regional High School in Bristol, NH** have worked to develop competencies which allow for more interdisciplinary work and thematic projects. Rather than using prescribed performance tasks for each competency, the NRHS model emphasizes that mastery can be shown in different ways, and students are given some choice in how they will demonstrate competency.

**Virtual Learning Academy Charter School** was the first NH statewide online school. Their courses are aligned to the NH state competencies. Students must show at least 85% proficiency in each course competency to pass a course. Targeted lessons help students master any specific competencies with which they are struggling.

**North Country Charter Academy** is an alternative high school that serves dropouts or students at-risk of dropping out. Most of the school curriculum is delivered using an online course provider. Students attend school sites at which they use the digital learning program, and move at a flexible pace with additional face-to-face support from teachers.

**Sanborn Regional High School** uses a competency based model in which students are given supports on an ongoing basis, with time set aside each day for catch up or acceleration of progress. Students who score below a certain level have the option to retake an exam to achieve mastery. Sanborn was one of the earliest schools in NH to adopt a competency based learning model.

**Lindsay Unified School District** is a high poverty and high ELL district in California. In response to many years of low achievement, LUSD defined the knowledge and skills required of Lindsay students in all content areas, and developed units of study for each learning standard in consultation with the Marzano Research Laboratory, Reinventing Schools Coalition, Rural Education for Americans Project, and Schwahn Leadership Associates. Beginning in 2009, the performance-based system was applied at the ninth grade, expanded to seventh to tenth grades in 2010, and then rolled out to include K-12. The LUSD design aims to meet learners at their level of instruction, allow learners to go back or move forward in any topic, and adopts an any-place any-time approach to learning. In 2012, LUSD won a $10 million Race to the Top grant.

Competency based learning is an essential part of **high school to career programming. The Advanced Technology Academy and the Advanced Photonic Academy, in Albuquerque, AZ.,** are examples. These academies are the focus of a collaboration between Sandia National Laboratories, Central New Mexico Community College, and the University of New Mexico.

**The Alamo Area Aerospace Academy** is a collaboration of businesses and school in San Antonio, and students spend half the day in high school and the other half learning aerospace maintenance, airframe and power plant mechanics, and other skill sets which may lead to employment or to continued education. In San Antonio, approximately 16% of Lockheed Martin's workforce is hired directly from the AAAA.

**Penn Medicine** teamed up with schools in the Philadelphia area to create the **Penn Medicine High School Pipeline Program.** This program enables students from lower socio-economic programs to choose among nursing, allied health care, or nonclinical healthcare tracks like finance or patient services, and offers incentives for students to enroll in continuing education after high school.

**The Academy for Technology Excellence in Ft. Myers, Florida,** was started as collaboration between Dunbar High School and local businesses including Microsoft, Chico's, First Community Bank, and other employers. Serving mostly students from poor households since 2005, the program trains students in 18 computer certifications and other skill areas, offers paid internships, and up to 48 postsecondary credits. Employers need skilled employees, and competency delivers rewarding jobs.

**Chugach School District** serves more than 200 students over a 20,000 square mile portion of south central Alaska. More than 70% of students are home-schoolers. In response to poor outcomes, in 1994 the district began a transition to competency based learning. Within five years, average student achievement on the California Achievement Test rose from the bottom quartile to the 72nd percentile. By 2000, student participation in college entrance exams rose from zero to more than 70%. **In 2001 CSD was given the prestigious Malcolm Baldrige National Quality Award** and in 2009 was selected as a recipient of the APEX Excellence Award. The story of Chugach is well told in *Delivering on the Promise* (2008), by Richard DeLorenzo, Wendy Battino, Rick Schreiber, and Barbara Gaddy-Carrio.

The CSD curriculum is based upon a continuum of standards in the ten content areas identified as essential. These essential content areas include mathematics, technology, social science, reading, writing, cultural awareness, personal/social/health, career development, service learning, and science. Each student has an individual learning plan, and advances through the key elements of each continuum at their own individual pace, aiming to meet or exceed the graduation level in each content area.

**As yet there is no consensus** regarding the key elements needed for a competency based high school graduation. New Hampshire has its defined competencies for graduation. The SCANS recommendations include five broadly defined competencies and three areas of foundation skill. The Hewlett Foundation's Deeper Learning framework identifies six interconnectedcompetencies essential for 21st century college and career readiness, including mastering core academic content, thinking critically and solving complex problems, working collaboratively, communicating effectively, learning how to learn, and develop academic mindsets. The EU identifies its *European Framework of Key Competences for Lifelong Learning*. Chugach recognizes ten continua as crucial for life after graduation. School to workplace programming identifies key skills for the worksites in a specific community.

This lack of consensus is an example of how different competency based learning is from the Taylorian "one best way" of curriculum-driven instruction. The key competencies for graduation are likely to be different in varied communities based on job opportunities, cultural differences, and the values of varied communities or families. The key competencies are likely to change with time as information, technology, economic factors, and shifts in patterns of affluence occur.

**We are at the beginning stages** of developing competency based learning systems with a focus on getting ready for life after high school. In spite of the incredible stranglehold curriculum-driven instruction has over most of our schools, innovators are finding ways to develop competency based systems to meet the needs of their students.

Moving forward in secondary schools, there are so many exciting competency based questions to consider:

- In your district or community, what are the crucial outcomes which will help young men and women become ready to live and work in our changing world?
- Should we create course-based or life skill-based outcomes?
- How do we measure competency for these crucial outcomes?
- How do we create specific pathways toward these competencies, and make each step clear and measurable?
- How do we train teachers to know their students learning needs and become facilitators of learning and development?
- How do we change a system that for more than a century has been designed to cover, test, and sort into a system that helps every student develop the skills to be an effective worker, learner and citizen?

## Competency Based Learning in Elementary and Pre-Schools

Historically, preschool and elementary educators have deeply appreciated the importance of educating the whole child. They have demonstrated awareness of the importance of sensory-motor skills and social-emotional skills. They have dedicated time and energy to relationship building, establishing a secure environment within the classroom, and practiced consistent classroom routines. Experienced early childhood educators understand the need to give instruction that offers students "just enough" challenge, but never so much that students become disengaged from learning.

But the curriculum-driven juggernaut of the last few decades has caused many schools to demand that early childhood and upper elementary classrooms **maintain the "rigorous" pace of instruction that ensures coverage** of every grade level content standard. As a result, many teachers have stepped away from instruction that better matches the needs of students, from giving attention to meeting the needs of the whole child, and from building a culture of trust and learning in the classroom.

> **Without a system in place to protect the development of crucial outcomes, many early childhood and elementary programs have become just another place where children race through content.**

In the process of trying to cover more content, we have trivialized deep understanding of essential content and skills and forgotten the importance of nurturing the whole child. In many schools, early childhood and upper elementary educators have succumbed to institutional pressures and surrendered to pacing guides and one-size-fits-all instructional programs. **During the vulnerable early childhood learning years, the effects of pushing kids into patterns of learning frustration are unconscionable.**

It is widely understood that by the end of third grade we can predict long-term learning outcomes for individual students with astounding accuracy (Annie E. Casey Foundation, 2010; Hernandez, 2011; Sornson, 2012; Snow et al., 1998; Torgeson, 1998; Torgeson, 2002). Yet in most schools/districts/states there has been no identification of and no system of tracking progress toward the crucial competencies that are the foundation for a lifetime of learning. Nonetheless, in every state and every community there are thoughtful educators lurking, waiting and watching for the opportunity to give young students the basic learning and social skills they need.

**Long-term learning success can be predicted by the end of third grade. Building a competency based early learning initiative does not focus on job readiness skills. Instead early childhood educators focus on the skills, concepts, and habits which allow children to become confident, skilled, motivated learners for life.**

In Kennewick, Washington, district staff identified a sequence of skill levels for the development of K-2 language arts skills including phonemic awareness, phonics, accuracy, fluency, and comprehension. As reported in *Annual Growth for All Students, Catch Up Growth for Those Who Are Behind* (Fielding et al., 2007), progress in these aspects of literacy development was carefully monitored, and students were then given instruction and practice time for each skill until it was mastered.

The Kennewick Schools are often cited as a model for **Response to Intervention** (RTI), which is conceptually a system for providing instruction to match the needs of each student and use systematic measurement of progress to make decisions about adjusting instruction.

RTI was identified in the 1997 Individuals with Disabilities Education Act as an alternative to using the severe discrepancy analysis to qualify for eligibility as an LD student, with the hope that early, diagnostic, explicit, and systematic interventions could help eliminate difficulties before they become entrenched.

Without clear standards for implementation, RTI initiatives vary widely in form and efficacy.

Successful RTI initiatives follow the principles of competency based learning by identifying a manageable set of crucial outcomes to be the focus of on-going assessment, gauging the learning needs of students to determine skill levels and readiness for instruction, developing an instructional plan, and monitoring progress toward essential outcomes. While RTI initiatives typically focus on at-risk students, competency based learning initiatives are designed to address the needs of all students.

> **Competency based early childhood and elementary educators are focused on the front end of the learning process, including the timely development of language skills, literacy, numeracy, sensory-motor, social-emotional and self-regulation skills.**

Timber Ridge (Grades 3-8) and Clover Ridge Schools (K-2), in Albany, Oregon have implemented standards-based instruction that includes a K-8 scope and sequence, explicit learning objectives, multi-age and subject integration, a personalized approach to learning, and a proficiency based report card.

The Maine School Administrative District 15 has developed Learning Target Maps for the elementary through high school sequence of skills in English Language Arts, Math, Science, Social Studies, Guidance, Health-Physical Education, Music, Technology and Engineering, Visual Arts, and World Language.

The Re-Inventing Schools Coalition (RISC) was established in 2002, based on the model that had been developed in the Chugach School District, and has worked to develop competency based systems in over 30 districts. Among these is Adams County School District 50, which decided to introduce competency based learning at the elementary level, believing that a systemic approach would reduce the frustration of older students who had not developed competencies required for graduation. In the fall of 2009, Adams 50 began its conversion to standards-based education. Adams has replaced grades with Levels 1–10 that incorporate standards from elementary school through high school graduation. Staff are working to develop standards for proficiency, assessment, and improving instruction. They are working with Educate to create an information system to track student progression.

The Early Learning Foundation was established in 2001, and uses *the Essential Skill Inventories, Preschool to Grade 3,* (Sornson, 2012) as its competency based framework during the early childhood years. Rather than focusing on literacy-only skills, the inventories include a set of crucial skills in all the domains of early childhood, including oral language, literacy, phonologic skills, numeracy, sensory-motor skills, behavior and self-regulation.

This whole child approach reflects the belief that these are all interrelated systems, that each domain contributes in its own way to long-term learning success. While grade level competencies set the framework for minimum expected outcomes, teachers are trained to focus on outcomes from a previous grade level or a more advanced level as needed. By systematically updating data on the inventory, teachers become trained to use observational assessment and to embed formative assessment into the design of instruction.

Simpson Central School, a K-8 school, was the pilot for the *Essential Skill Inventories* in Simpson County, and began implementation of this competency model in 2008–09. They began with implementation in Kindergarten, and gradually phased in First and Second Grade. Staff learned to:

- Clearly identify essential learning outcomes in all the domains of early childhood.
- Use systematic assessment to determine the readiness levels of students in relation to essential outcomes.
- Offer informed instruction and carefully monitor progress until these skills/objectives are deeply understood (competency).
- Advance students to higher-level work upon demonstration of mastery.

The district aligned report cards with the inventories, which encouraged staff to help parents understand the concept of crucial learning outcomes, and to see more specifically what students were being asked to learn well. As part of an evaluation of improved teacher behaviors based on the use of this competency based learning model, **teachers reported significant improvements in their teaching skills and behaviors** associated with early learning success (Sornson, 2015). In 2007–08, before beginning this process, 37% of Simpson Central third grader scored at proficient or above on the state's reading tests and 59% did so in math. In 2013–14, student outcomes had improved to almost 64% in reading and just over 86% in math (Sornson & Davis, 2013).

At the beginning of the 2014–15 school year **Simpson Central School was rated as a Mississippi "A" level school, an extraordinary achievement for a high poverty school.** Teachers often refer to the essential skills as the "core of the core" because they describe those skills that cannot be overlooked if these children are to find the path to long-term learning success.

The digital revolution has not been lost on developers of early childhood learning products. Learning games, language and reading programs, math learning systems, digital home schooling models, video-game learning environments, digital learning with social networking, and more are part of the landscape of products for sale. Increasingly, toy, media, and product producers are exploring the early childhood learning market. The types and uses of technology in early childhood programs have expanded to include computers, tablets, e-books, mobile devices, handheld gaming devices, digital cameras and video camcorders, electronic toys, multimedia players for music and videos, digital audio recorders, interactive whiteboards, software applications, the Internet, streaming media, and more.

Everyone from the largest international education materials producers to small teams of app producers are looking for a portion of this digital learning market, and building products that incorporate scaffolding, clear learning objectives, internal tracking of success, assessment of progress, diagnostic reports, and data management. Digital competency based learning programs for both home and school are available. Some technology producers, like Dr. Dan Yang, founder of VINCI Education and the VINCI Virtual School, see systematic digital early childhood learning systems as a vehicle for closing the achievement gap and maximizing development in the early years.

Other education early childhood leaders express concern with the overuse of technology, the lack of interactive language, social, and physical experience, and the lack of hands on parent and caregiver involvement in the learning of young children. Thoughtful use of digital learning systems, blended systems, and technology to track progress along the pathways to major competencies in life is inevitable.

While digital options are increasingly available, **some early learning skills require hands-on and three dimensional learning.** The *Essential Math Skills* (Sornson, 2014) offers a sequence of 29 preschool to grade 3 math skills which are at the core of number sense and deep understanding of early math. A menu of hands-on or movement based activities for each skill is suggested for each skill, but teachers and parents are encouraged to develop variations or additional activities.

This pathway to early math competency is not intended to be a lesson by lesson one-size-fits-all learning program. Instead it is a guide to help teachers track progress toward competency for each student while providing many activity options for instruction in small groups, activity centers, or individualized learning. Unlike a digital program that adjusts the task for you, this early math skill competency framework puts teachers/parents in the role of instructional planner. Teachers are in charge of assessing student readiness, picking appropriate activities, monitoring progress, allowing more practice time or moving students forward to higher levels of challenge. **With proficiency in these 29 math skills, students deeply understand and can apply basic number concepts,** and are prepared for more advanced traditional or digital learning math learning opportunities.

**It is just as important to develop high-quality pathways to competency during the early learning years as at any other level. These are the foundational years, in which patterns of success, love of learning, and habits of mind are developed. These are the years during which the cover, test, sort educational model does the greatest harm. If we can help children develop solid basic skills while falling in love with learning, we will have improved the lives of our children and the future of our society.**

**The continued use of a coverage-driven model of learning is causing many young children to become discouraged and disengaged from learning. Poor or otherwise disadvantaged children pay an inordinately heavy cost.** These kids are more likely to struggle to keep up with the pace of instruction, far more likely to become unsuccessful learners, and in time they are far more likely to end up with low skill low wage jobs. If we ever honestly hope to level the playing field and give all children an opportunity to succeed in the information society, it will require a transition from one-size-fits-all instruction to a new model based on respect for the differences among us and the inherent potential in us all.

The transition to a competency model allows us to systematically offer every child the opportunity to become a lifelong learner. Moving to a competency based model allows us to consider the needs of the whole child, in all the domains of early childhood, including oral language, literacy, phonologic skills, numeracy, sensory-motor skills, behavior and self-regulation.

In the competency based early learning environments of the future, pathways to success will be built with explicit and measurable learning objectives rather than long lists of things to race through so they are covered. Students will advance upon mastery, not be pushed along with the class without considering readiness. Assessment will be primarily formative, its purpose being to help the teacher know how to adjust instruction, rather than judging and ranking kids with schools.

**Competency based learning systems at the preschool and elementary school levels have the potential to give far more students a chance to become successful learners for life.** Identifying essential early learning outcomes, and building pathways to help children achieve these outcomes at their own rate of readiness, are the challenge and the opportunity of our time.

# 15

# Teacher Education: Building Pathways to Skills That Matter

The enthusiastic attention given to competency based learning in some education sectors has not yet been matched by our teacher education programs. Credits based on seat time continue to be the way to earn teaching degrees. Because of a general mistrust of the quality of skills associated with teacher education program completion, most states also require candidates to pass a standardized test (such as the Praxis Exam, the National Evaluation Series, or the Professional Readiness Examination) for licensure.

Requirements for teacher certification vary on a state-by-state basis. Some states have specific credit and course requirements, while others allow state approved teacher education programs to set the standards for their institution. No states have yet established clear competencies, replacing traditional credit requirements, which would describe what you must know and be able to do as a prerequisite for teaching.

> The CEU system used for continued teacher and administrator certification is a vivid example of our reliance on the time-based model.

In Michigan, 150 State Continuing Education Clock Hours (SCECHs) within three years allows you to renew your provisional certificate. In New York, to maintain a professional certificate a teacher can complete 175 hours of professional development every five years. In California, licenses can be renewed without verification of any professional development hours, although districts are required to offer a program of professional development of at least 18 hours.

In Oklahoma, 75 clock hours over a five-year period allows you to renew your professional certificate.

Any warm body can earn CEUs. If you are present, and remember to sign in and sign out, you earn your contact hours. The quality of instruction is not considered. Learning outcomes are not considered. Application of learning is not considered.

The National Board for Professional Teaching Standards stands out as an exception to the continued emphasis on seat time and credits, and was among the first voices for setting standards for teacher competency. This organization has developed standards for NBPTS certification in 25 certificate areas such as elementary art, high school English language arts, middle school math, etc. Experienced educators voluntarily seeking National Board certification go through a rigorous process to demonstrate their capacity to meet or exceed the standards. Since 1987, more than 110,000 teachers in the United States have achieved certification.

The United Nations Educational, Scientific and Cultural Organization (UNESCO) ICT-CST project, working with Microsoft, Intel, Cisco, the International Society for Technology in Education (ISTE), and the Virginia Polytechnic Institute and State University (Virginia Tech), has developed a matrix of skills to help educational policy-makers and curriculum developers identify the skills teachers need to harness technology in the service of education. The projects' *ICT Competency Standards for Teachers, Implementation Guidelines* (United Nations, 2008) identifies specific learning objectives for teachers and a suggested standard for how this could be applied in the classroom for technology literacy, knowledge deepening, and knowledge creation.

The Buros Center for Testing (1990), working with the American Federation of Teachers, the National Council on Measurement in Education, and the National Education Association, developed *Standards for Teacher Competence in Educational Assessment of Students.* These standards call on educators to demonstrate skill at selecting, developing, applying, using, communicating, and evaluating student assessment information and student assessment practices.

- Teachers should be skilled in choosing assessment methods appropriate for instructional decisions.
- Teachers should be skilled in developing assessment methods appropriate for instructional decisions.
- The teacher should be skilled in administering, scoring and interpreting the results of both externally produced and teacher-produced assessment methods.
- Teachers should be skilled in using assessment results when making decisions about individual students, planning teaching, developing curriculum, and school improvement.
- Teachers should be skilled in developing valid pupil grading procedures which use pupil assessments.
- Teachers should be skilled in communicating assessment results to students, parents, other lay audiences, and other educators.
- Teachers should be skilled in recognizing unethical, illegal, and otherwise inappropriate assessment methods and uses of assessment information.

The International Association for K-12 Online Learning (iNACOL, 2014) has developed a framework of competencies for blended learning. *iNACOL Blended Learning Teacher Competency Framework* describes a set of competencies under the headings of Mindsets, Qualities, Adaptive Skills, and Technical Skills.

The Teacher Leadership Consortium (2014) has developed its *Teacher Leader Model Standards* to guide the preparation of experienced teachers to assume leadership roles. These standards describe a set of skills in seven domains, including:

- Fostering a collaborative culture to support educator development and student learning.
- Accessing and using research to improve practice and student learning.
- Promoting professional learning for continuous improvement.
- Facilitating improvements in instruction and student learning.
- Promoting the use of assessments and data for school and district improvement.
- Improving outreach and collaboration with families and community.
- Advocating for student learning and the profession.

The Council of Chief State School Officers (CCSSO) and its Interstate Teacher Assessment and Support Consortium (inTASC) have created the *Model Core Teaching Standards and Learning Progressions for Teachers 1.0* (2013). These standards are described as the teaching competencies needed across all grade levels and subject areas for a transformed public education system. The CCSSO recommends ten standards and a learning progression for each standard:

- Standard #1: Learner Development. The teacher understands how learners grow and develop, recognizing that patterns of learning and development vary individually within and across the cognitive, linguistic, social, emotional, and physical areas, and designs and implements developmentally appropriate and challenging learning experiences.
- Standard #2: Learning Differences. The teacher uses understanding of individual differences and diverse cultures and communities to ensure inclusive learning environments that enable each learner to meet high standards.
- Standard #3: Learning Environments. The teacher works with others to create environments that support individual and collaborative learning, and that encourage positive

social interaction, active engagement in learning, and self-motivation.
- Standard #4: Content Knowledge. The teacher understands the central concepts, tools of inquiry, and structures of the discipline(s) he or she teaches and creates learning experiences that make the discipline accessible and meaningful for learners to assure mastery of the content.
- Standard #5: Application of Content. The teacher understands how to connect concepts and use differing perspectives to engage learners in critical thinking, creativity, and collaborative problem-solving related to authentic local and global issues.
- Standard #6: Assessment. The teacher understands and uses multiple methods of assessment to engage learners in their own growth, to monitor learner progress, and to guide the teacher's and learner's decision-making.
- Standard #7: Planning for Instruction. The teacher plans instruction that supports every student in meeting rigorous learning goals by drawing upon knowledge of content areas, curriculum, cross-disciplinary skills, and pedagogy, as well as knowledge of learners and the community context.
- Standard #8: Instructional Strategies. The teacher understands and uses a variety of instructional strategies to encourage learners to develop deep understanding of content areas and their connections, and to build skills to apply knowledge in meaningful ways.
- Standard #9: Professional Learning and Ethical Practice. The teacher engages in ongoing professional learning and uses evidence to continually evaluate his/her practice, particularly the effects of his/her choices and actions on others (learners, families, other professionals, and the community), and adapts practice to meet the needs of each learner.
- Standard #10: Leadership and Collaboration. The teacher seeks appropriate leadership roles and opportunities

to take responsibility for student learning, to collaborate with learners, families, colleagues, other school professionals, and community members to ensure learner growth, and to advance the profession.

**The National Association of Elementary School Principals** (2014) has called for principals to achieve six school leadership competencies in support of the development of high-quality early learning from age three to grade three. The framework for these Pre-K to Grade 3 administrative competencies includes:

- Embrace the Pre-K-3 Early Learning Continuum. Effective principals embrace a concept of high-quality early learning from age three to grade three as the foundation for children's developmental growth.
- Ensure Developmentally-Appropriate Teaching. Effective principals ensure quality teaching, supported by a system of standards, developmentally appropriate curriculum, and assessments that work together to help foster children's learning and growth.
- Provide Personalized, Blended Learning Environments. Effective principals provide welcoming, collaborative learning environments that support personalized learning, including the effective use of technology.
- Use Multiple Measures to Guide Growth in Student Learning. Effective principals use multiples measures to assess student progress and support student learning growth.
- Build Professional Capacity Across the Learning Community. Effective principals build collaborative working environments that support the professional growth of all who work in them.
- Make Your School a Hub of Pre-K-3 Learning for Families and Communities. Effective principals work with families, prekindergarten programs, and community organizations to build strong Pre-K-3 linkages. Effective principals work with families, prekindergarten programs, and community organizations to build strong Pre-K-3 linkages.

While the NAESP document does a good job of offering a general description of six leadership areas, it has not yet established rubrics that clarify exactly what competency looks like in each area. Nor has the NAESP led the way to a training program that would help aspiring leaders develop these skills.

> **These examples reflect the beginning stages of considering and then building competency frameworks for educator development. Under the curriculum-driven CTS model, the expectation for teachers was simple: manage behavior and cover the content. Without a sense of urgency that all students succeed the coverage-based teacher training model sufficed. Finding the best teacher candidates, ensuring that each teacher-in-training developed a set of crucial skills, and then offering continued on the job training to reach higher levels of skill and professionalism was not considered essential.**

Some schools are **not waiting for state or university teacher training requirements to change,** and have already taken steps to define the competencies more specifically. These efforts to clearly **define the skills and knowledge crucial for professional classroom educator success** is in its early stages, and there is great opportunity for innovation among schools who can more specifically define what they want teachers to know and be able to do, create personalized learning pathways, and set standards for demonstration of competence in every crucial teaching skill.

**The Summit Public Schools** is one example of a district which has blended evaluation with planned learning to improve teacher skills. Summit is a system of 7 charter middle and high schools headquartered in Redwood City, California, which measures teachers using seven categories: assessment, content, curriculum, instruction, knowing learners and learning, leadership, and mentoring. Depending on how well they can demonstrate their expertise in each of these areas, teachers are placed at one of four levels: basic, proficient, highly proficient, and expert. Every teacher participates in at least 40 days of professional development per year, which is designed to mirror the self-directed learning model used with Summit students.

> **As we realize the importance of helping lots more students become successful lifelong learners, we have reached a tipping point. Failure to help children learn well inflicts incredible costs both to students and to society. The efficacy of instruction matters. We have reached the point at which we are beginning to realize that the skills of our teachers are just as important as the skills of nurses, doctors, electricians, tech workers, plumbers and accountants. Teacher competency matters.**

**Competency based teacher education requires a new starting point.** Instead of preparing a curriculum or course plan by identifying content and/or required reading, a competency based teacher development program begin by **identifying essential competencies**. Teacher training institutions and/or states are challenged to:

- Develop a competency map for what teachers should know and be able to do. The map can be specific to your state/community's learning needs, and the needs of differing roles within the education community. The crucial competencies must be spelled out clearly.
- Develop pathways to your crucial competencies, the steps which lead to your desired outcomes.
- Develop clear rubrics and reliable assessments of competency for each and every step along the pathway.
- Ensure that individual educators are included in the development of personalized plans to develop each competency.
- Allow individual educators to include learning goals in their personalized plan which exceed competency in some areas.
- Assess the learning needs of teacher candidates.

- Develop training systems which include personalization based on the learning needs of each student-educator.
- Develop cohort and on-line support systems for developing educators.
- Identify existing resources which match the identified learning needs.
- Find or develop instructional options which are missing from present-day teacher education programs.
- Use demonstrated competence rather than courses and credits to certify teachers.
- Work with school districts and other institutions to develop post-certification training programs to support educators who wish to achieve higher levels of competency.

# 16

# Distracted By the Debate Over What to Cover

The Common Core State Standards **are not a competency framework,** which describe discrete learning objectives and the pathway of skills leading to higher level skills. **CCSS are a framework for coverage,** describing those areas of content which are recommended for inclusion in the curriculum. The Texas Essential Knowledge and Skills standards (TEKS) are a **coverage framework,** as are the Indiana Academic Standards and every other set of state grade-level content standards. Across the nation, these "standards" as we know them are a list of things to cover or include in the instructional plan, offering a general map of what can be taught at the different grades and ages.

For several years after the emergence of the Common Core State Standards there was a political debate over whether to cover this set of coverage standards (CCSS), or some different or modified set of standards for coverage. But with the pressure of required annual testing, most states settled into a pattern of using something close to CCSS so that they could arguably "cover" most of the material that might be included on the standardized one-size-fits-all annual assessment.

> **And so most schools have continued to march to the same drummer. One set of coverage standards for each grade. One standardized assessment for each grade. Too much content to cover in the time available, and the pressure of using a pacing guide to get it all covered.**

More than a hundred years after Frederick Winslow Taylor described his management principles in the book *The Principles of Scientific Management* (1911), today's CCSS debate demonstrates how we continue to search for "the one best way" of standardized instruction.

"*What are we going to cover, and how are we going to test it?*" are questions from the old Prussian, Taylorized, curriculum-driven, summative test-driven school model which has failed us for far too long, and is now experiencing its death throes.

**As we begin down the road of developing systems based on competency based learning, let's hope that no one claims to have "the one best way" for a very long time. There is so much to learn about competency based learning models that work.**

There are many and differing ideas of what we want a high school graduate to know and be able to do. We've barely begun the development of pathways to competency, and arguable are beginning to see that there can be multiple pathways to competency. School to work initiatives are growing, but will change each decade with the evolving demands of the workplace. Higher education has just begun to compete for students in a competency driven environment. Technology gives us opportunities for individualized learning, digital learning, free learning options, and blended learning. And as competency based learning options become available, families can also play an even greater role in the development of their children.

# 17

# Letting Go of Curriculum-Driven Instruction

For many years we've equated being a good teacher with preparing lesson plans and then delivering them well. Teachers have been asked to turn in lesson plans every week, noting the state or national standards covered in each day's plan. We've worked on committees to develop pacing guides and district quarterly assessments to ensure that everyone is keeping up with the plan for coverage. Our curriculum maps have been remodeled to fit the CCSS. We've purchased learning programs and textbooks which claim to cover all the standards, if only we can keep up the pace of instruction. We're up to our ears in alligators. Leave us alone!

The implementation of competency based learning will **elicit resistance** for all the usual human reasons. Here are just a few:

## Safety

There is safety in the familiar. With our years of training and well-refined skills in curriculum-driven instruction, there is an element of danger in changing to a model in which the demands and expectations are different.

## Mental Models

As children we developed a mental model of what it is to be a teacher. For me, Sister Mary Bruno, Mr. Mitrano, and Mrs. Larsen were inspiring representations of what it means to be a teacher.

Within the stand and deliver model of instruction, they were brilliant models. Finding wonderful models of competency based learning is still a challenge.

## Comfortable Routines

On Sunday night we sit on the porch and write lessons for the week. For years this has been the routine. And now someone wants us to prepare learning plans based on identified crucial outcomes, knowing our students, providing instruction matched to their specific learning needs, also providing some group activities for exploration, exposure, and general knowledge. The old way was simpler, more familiar, and more comfortable.

## Effort

Years ago we developed high-quality lesson plans, and then we refined them over the years so that all the new content expectations were also being covered. We have study guides and tests all prepared that go along with those lessons. Now you want us to become the guide on the side instead of the sage on the stage. You want us to abandon the lesson plans on which we have spent countless hours.

## Limitations on Personal Responsibility

To some degree we all put limits on taking personal responsibility for another person's effort and learning. Competency based learning creates the clear expectation that crucial outcomes must be learned to deep understanding and application. Teachers might be fearful of being held to that standard. This is partly because they have not fully realized that if students have clear learning goals and are given instruction at their level, with the understanding that competency precedes moving on, students' ownership of their own learning will be vastly improved.

## One More Thing

Many experienced teachers have seen the new educational fads coming around every few years. They might easily assume that CBL is just another fad, and will fade away in a few years like so many other programs or buzzwords.

## Perceived Status

Some staff members have worked for years to gain a sense of respect from their colleagues, or in their community. Any significant change initiative threatens familiar roles and the perception of status.

## Lack of Skills and Training

Please don't put me in the pilot's seat of an airplane without first giving me quality training. Educators who do not understand instructional match, have seldom used formative assessment, and are not yet familiar with systematic observational assessment will be justly afraid of the demands of competency based learning.

## Lack of Trust

When educators feel they cannot trust each other or key school decision makers, it is hard to accept change. When you are in a fear-based organizational culture you resist new ideas. Trust is a necessary component for optimal thinking, listening, collaboration, and problem-solving.

## Good Excuses for Low Expectations

Competency requires clear high standards for crucial learning outcomes. Some teachers who are used to the coverage model will find ways to excuse low performance and try to certify students as competent even when they are not. *He tries so hard. She brought in brownies for extra credit. Her parents are such nice people.* Likewise administrators want their teachers to be successful, and some will find ways to pretend that consistent formative assessment or high-quality differentiated instruction are happening in the classroom.

## We Are Way Too Busy

When we are asked to do something new, difficult, or not yet fully understood, some folks will find ways to avoid it. Just as we fill up our day with busy work when we are avoiding some chore at home, some educators will find that the day was far too busy to get around to data collection, individual planning, or other important aspects of CBL.

## The Kids Love Me Just as I Am

There are many reasons to justify resisting change, and this one is a classic. Teachers who have managed to somehow get kids to love them even while they are delivering one-size-fits-all instruction can certainly get kids to love them when they start to deliver high-quality competency based instruction.

## Our School is Doing Fine without CBL

In most cases schools look for new ideas only when they see a need. Chugach, New Hampshire, and Simpson County Schools wanted to vastly improve their outcomes. Occasionally a successful school with some extraordinary leaders (including teacher leaders) will look for a better way. Some schools will resist CBL by clinging to the belief that they are already doing everything that can possibly be done to serve their students.

## We Are Already Doing Competency

Some school leaders have the most amazing capacity to believe/say they are already doing every new thing that comes along in the world of education. Whole child learning, differentiated instruction, response to intervention, constructivism, nature learning, learning styles, multiple intelligences, personalized learning, blended learning, home-school connections, scaffolding, early intervention, socio-emotional learning, character development, and competency. *Oh yes, we are already doing that.*

## Money and Power

Competency based learning offers efficiencies which could reduce some of the unnecessary costs of our highly bureaucratic and educationally inept systems. Nonetheless there are powerful financial and political interests which will protect the status quo.

One-size-fits-all assessment systems, textbooks, workbooks, and other learning materials won't stand the test of a competency driven system. They will need to be adapted to the different design needs of a competency driven system. The designers, distributors, and monitors of rigid pacing guides will abhor the individualization that comes with competency systems. Politicians and bureaucrats who favor overly simplistic one-size-fits-all regulations will find a way to not understand the need for change toward a more effective, respectful, and joyful way of teaching and learning.

Change can be seen as both an opportunity and a crisis. For every teacher who embraces competency based learning as an opportunity to meet the needs of each student, there will be others who resist giving up familiar lessons plans and worksheets. For every administrator who has longed for a better way to create respectful environments for learning and schools where teachers love to teach, there will be others who hold on to familiar patterns and do not want to do the challenging work of recreating systems of learning. For every politician who actually reads the research, and understands how much we need thoughtful planning toward a more effective system of training our children to compete in a global society, there will be others who cling to political posturing from the past. For every entrepreneur who sees the opportunity to develop new learning products and systems, there are huge international companies with political clout who are trying to hold onto existing market share.

**The logistics of making the change to competency based learning are not as daunting as they might seem.**

The model is here, all around us. The resources, the experience of trailbreakers, and expert guidance are available. **Every principle of good teaching and learning supports the practice of competency based learning.** Teachers and administrators urgently want to be part of a system that succeeds for kids, in which they get to be professionals and work within a respectful and collaborative environment. Parents and community leaders are clamoring for the changes that will help their children be intellectually and emotionally ready to succeed in the modern world.

**Resistance is a natural part of change,** within individuals and within our business, political, and educational systems.

We can't wish it gone, or push it away. With resolve and compassion, those who embrace the opportunity to create competency based learning systems can overcome these predictable patterns and build learning systems in which the highest standards for learning, teaching, empathy, and character flourish.

# 18

# Transitioning from Curriculum-Driven to Competency Based Learning

Those schools, school districts, colleges, preschools, publishers, technology innovators, thinkers, and community members who choose to lead the transformation toward competency based learning systems will face many challenges. We are redesigning an airplane that is in flight.

We can't shut down the schools and just study all this for a few years. There are millions of young men and women in the process of being educated today. None of that stops. No timeouts. The transformation to competency based learning will emerge from the curriculum-driven systems in which we now operate.

> For those who are ready to innovate, this will be the most exciting time in the history of education. We have barely scratched the surface of the potential for human learning. Decades of discovery and transformation lie ahead. We need thoughtful educators, parents, and community leaders to create pathways to knowledge and competent skills that matter.

New systems of defining the expertise and instruction needed for highly skilled jobs are waiting to be developed. The skills needed for high school completion must be redefined, and will likely look different from place to place. The basic structure of high schools will be reconsidered. It is unlikely that all students need to take the same courses or develop the same skill sets to be successful in the world.

The foundation skills needed in the early years of learning have only recently been mapped, and the many ways to help children develop these skills will be reconceptualized by innovative educators and parents. One-size-fits-all learning programs are unlikely to persist, **and a new generation of Montessoris, Steiners, Vygotskys, and Ericksons will lead us** to consider better systems of learning to meet the needs of modern learners.

Digital, blended, hands-on, and socially interactive learning systems will be developed to bring learning alive for more students, to extend learning so that learning is truly possible anywhere, anytime, and at any pace.

**The excitement of creating new systems may bring back** those gifted individuals we so desperately need to public and private education. Be an educator. From the ashes of decades of school reform failure will emerge the Phoenix of education systems that bring learning alive for our children.

It is already happening. From Alaska to New Hampshire, from universities to preschools, there is recognition that **competency matters,** and that we can design systems that allow far more students become successful learners for life. The years of transition ahead of us will be filled with innovation and experimentation, mistakes, and discoveries. Consider these ideas as you create high-quality competency based systems in your school or community.

**Take time** for preliminary planning, knowing that the process of transformation will last for years. Too often in education we adopt the newest standards without having an opportunity to even read them, or embrace a new instructional program without carefully planning for the rollout challenges. Pick thoughtful contributors to this study process who represent all stakeholder groups, and allow them to do meaningful work. Examine the change from as many different perspectives as possible. Build a clear consensus around the need for transformation.

**Pick a point of beginning,** whether it is high school graduation requirements, certificate completion competencies, or early childhood essential outcomes. Decide on the competencies or outcomes that are essential, and make sure these are described precisely. Coverage standards can be vague; competencies must be crystal clear.

**Design the competency based learning architecture, Version 1.0.** This design starts with:

- Clear competencies which articulate exactly what students need to know and be able to do.
- Specific steps along the pathways to competency.
- Rubrics that describe the standards for proficiency/competency/mastery at each step.
- The development, purchase, and/or adaptation of an instructional plan and instructional materials organized around the competencies.
- Assessment systems (formative and summative) that are consistent and reliable
- The role of technology for instruction.
- The role of technology for assessment.
- Opportunities for students to help choose learning goals above minimum expectations.
- The role of the student to help design pathways to competency which match interests and learning style.
- Home-school partnerships which allow parent input and to the development of learning plans and participation in the learning process.
- Systems to communicate progress toward competency in the required and chosen learning goals.
- Short term and on-going staff and community training needs.

**Develop a three to five year plan for implementation.** Set milestones to track progress in each essential element of the plan, and create systems to track advancement toward each milestone. If it is possible, plan on implementing change in phases. This will allow you to work out any problems that emerge in the process.

**Form a transition team to monitor and ensure progress.** Recruit stakeholders from all parts of the system/school. Teacher leaders and other employees who have the respect of the staff should be part of the transition team. Gather support for the change from all school leaders, including those who are not part of management. Make sure that the initiative is not seen as the product of a small group of visionaries, and that it is not seen as one more thing that will disappear in two to three years.

**Begin training staff long before implementing the preliminary roll out.** You can choose to train only those employees that will be affected first, or you can train all employees that will eventually be affected. Remember that training is more than "coverage'. Helping staff develop competency in all the skills and understandings needed for CBL will include significant training over time.

**Develop teacher leaders.** Individual coaching and peer mentoring models can be helpful with reluctant staff members who might procrastinate, miss deadlines, or avoid the significant learning needed to become a successful competency based instructor. By working side by side with a peer who can encourage, clarify, and help them keep pace with the change process can make individuals feel more like a part of a team.

**Become a learning organization.** Most educators will need to develop new skills to enable them to succeed in this new model of learning. Some of these skills include, but are not limited to:

- Aligning instruction to the explicit, measurable learning objectives that make up the pathway to competency.
- Providing timely, differentiated support to students based on individual learning needs, moving each student along an individual learning pathway at a sufficient pace to achieve essential learning goals.

- Using formative and summative assessments to regularly assess student progress.
- Developing and implement performance-based formative and summative assessments with high validity and reliability.
- Collaborating with other staff members for the development and implementation of assessment and instructional plans.
- Using data on individual student learning in a timely, ongoing manner to inform instruction and support student progress to competency.
- Supporting development of the whole child/student including social and emotional competencies.
  - Designing and managing personalized instruction using technology, blended or online learning, and other options.
  - Working with students to get input on student learning goals or a plan for pathways to competency.
  - Working with parents to build strong partnerships supporting the development of competency.

**Clear the obstacles to implementation.** Identify employees or community leaders that may cause obstacles to the transition, and work with them. Identify resource issues which could interfere with your plan's implementation or success.

**Plan the transition.** Allow the transition team to give input before crafting a final implementation plan. Create a comprehensive plan detailing how the transition will take place, how it will affect each group of stakeholders, and the timetable for the change. The transition team should present the plan to the school and community with confidence, and the plan must be clear enough for everyone to understand the vision.

**Put the transition plan on paper** so everyone knows the blueprint for change. This plan should explain why the change is being made and what the school will look like when the transition is complete.

**Proceed one step at a time.** While many of us may be frustrated by the slow pace of change, the creation of a competency based learning system must be done well. Rushing through the plan sounds a lot like rushing through instruction. Take your time, help people along, ensure understanding, experiment, innovate, learn from your mistakes, and enjoy the process of creating meaningful change that will last.

# 19

# Informed Instruction Leads to Competency, Part Two

**Curriculum-driven instruction** is based on one set of concepts or thought patterns. Teachers cover material at a specified pace. Tests are given to assess how well students understood the material. The teacher then moves forward to cover new material. Successful students keep up with the pace of instruction. Successful students advance toward higher levels of learning.

Rigor is related to covering more content. Less successful students are screened into classes and careers which require less learning. **A large majority of students will fall into patterns of disengagement from learning.** Education experts develop content expectations which teachers are expected to cover. District summative assessment systems, digital assessment systems, and state assessment systems are in place to ensure coverage and judge the success of schools and teachers.

> Cover, test, and sort worked well enough in the 19th and early 20th centuries. But in today's world it is a greater burden to be an unsuccessful learner, as this leads to a life of low-skill and low-wage employment opportunities.

**Competency based learning is driven by a different set of premises.** Lifelong learning is an essential ingredient for personal, social, and economic success. People learn best when important instruction is given at the student's readiness level. Students should move on to higher levels of learning when they are fully ready. Essential learning outcomes must be clear and compelling. Pathways to competency show the steps which build up to high-level competencies. Instructors should know each student's level of readiness, and deliver crucial instruction at thatlevel. Children learn at different rates and in different ways. Given the necessary time and instruction, almost all students can achieve competency in important language, social-emotional, motor, literacy, and numeracy skills needed for a foundation of learning success. Given the necessary time and instruction, almost all students can advance along the pathways to competency which will allow them access to the job skills which can support personal success. Learning can occur anywhere, at any time of day, and at any pace.

Learning models are informed by their premises. No reasonable person argues that all students learn in the same way or at the same pace. Yet rigid pacing guides abound in our schools. It is part of the basic paradigm, the thought pattern for how we do things, the patterns we accept without careful scrutiny.

When Vygotsky, Betts, Gickling, or Burns described the importance of *instructional match*, most educators understood its importance. But nothing much changed in the schools. When Schmoker and Marzano called for *standards that are clear, not confusing; essential, not exhaustive*, we wholeheartedly agreed. But our patterns of instruction persisted. When DuFour and Eacker articulated the first key question of PLCs, *What do we expect students to learn*, we celebrated this wisdom. But again nothing changed. As John Hattie urged us to *clarify what students must learn* as the first step for a successful learning strategy, we acknowledged this obvious truth, but most schools have not yet acted upon this research.

> **Throughout this book we have explored a set of simple ideas about teaching and learning. Identify crucial learning outcomes. Find out what your students can do, and what they are ready to learn. For crucial outcomes, plan instruction based on a student's instructional level. Deliver informed instruction for as long as it takes until the outcome is well learned. Move students along when they are ready. Competency matters.**

Despite the research, most educators go to work and give great energy to perpetuating the old model. **We cling to what we know.** The boat is leaking, and we know how to patch leaks, and we do so with vigor. We may be so busy patching that we never look up long enough to see that a new vessel is there, waiting to be discovered.

The Cover Test Sort educational model was informed by long lists of grade level content standards and pacing guides. Teachers were asked to race through nonviable content at breakneck speed, and then judged to have failed when students were not able to successfully perform on summative assessments. With kids struggling and teachers struggling, there was too much failure to go around.

**A new model is emerging.** It is designed with an understanding of the importance of learning success. It is built to help students achieve clear and crucial learning goals. It is informed by a solid understanding of a child's readiness for learning, and by the commitment to give students what they need at their instructional level of as long as it takes. Its architecture includes pathways to competency, sometimes different for one student than another. In this model, learning is for life, and must be based on the joyful engagement of the learner.

# 20
# Conclusion: The Spirit of Transformation

One-size-fits-all education systems no longer serve the needs of individuals or of society. While transformational change has already occurred in science and technology, and while new ideas and new business models emerge at unprecedented rates, our institutions of education have been astonishingly successful at resisting change, until now. In a world of innovation and information, we are responsible to help our children develop the foundation skills, the habits of learning, and a powerful understanding that they can be learners for life.

> Those of us who are educators, parents, and community leaders have the information, tools, and opportunity to create an educational process which works for many more students, a process which respects diversity, embraces personalization, and continuously improves.

We live in an era of transformation. At no time in history has there been more scientific inquiry, information, technology, freedom, and capacity for change. **In the past hundred years change has become the constant,** affecting every aspect of the way we live and work.

At Kitty Hawk, North Carolina on December 17, 1903, the Wright brothers achieved the first sustained flight with a powered, controlled aircraft. Orville Wright was the pilot of the first flight of 120 feet in 12 seconds. In the fourth flight of the same day, Wilbur Wright flew 852 feet in 59 seconds. The age of air travel had begun, and human ingenuity is hard to restrain.

From those first precarious flights came an astonishing sequence of innovations. In less than 66 years space flight accomplished the unimaginable. On July 20, 1969, Neil Armstrong and Buzz Aldrin became the first humans to step onto the surface of the moon. They spent about two and a half hours on the moon, rejoined Michael Collins on the command spacecraft, which was in lunar orbit, and returned to Earth. We've begun to explore the unfathomable limits of space. Soon there will be manned visits to Mars.

Beginning in the mid-19th century, generations of woman suffrage supporters lectured, wrote, marched, lobbied, and practiced civil disobedience to secure the basic right to vote and run for office. What seemed like a radical idea to some became the law of the land, finally passed by Congress in 1919 and ratified on August 18, 1920. The transformation away from gender based limitations has begun.

In the United States slavery was legal in all thirteen colonies at the inception of our country. By 1850 there were four million slaves in our country. The Civil War effectively ended slavery and the thirteenth amendment to the Constitution was formally approved in 1865. Even then Jim Crow segregation laws limited access to schools and public facilities for many black Americans. Anti-miscegenation laws prohibited whites and blacks from marrying each other. Voting rights were limited in some states. Black servicemen often served in segregated units. Jackie Robinson joined the Brooklyn Dodgers in 1947, beginning a pattern of change in sports. In December 1955 Rosa Parks refused to go the back of the bus in Montgomery, Alabama. Not until 1968 did the Civil Rights Act ban discrimination in the sale and rental of homes.

Discrimination based on race is now illegal.

Satellites roam our skies, bringing us information and entertainment. We talk to our phones, and they guide us turn by turn as we travel. The smartphone in your pocket has more computing power than the entire National Aeronautics and Space Administration (NASA) when astronauts completed the moon mission. We can search for information on any topic with astonishing speed. Diseases which once ravaged the planet have been eliminated or diminished. Many of us safely travel tens of thousands of miles through the air each year. We've mapped the human genome, and discovered the human microbiome. **Surely we have the capacity to personalize learning, track progress, and challenge students at the level that optimizes success.**

The clamor for school reform over the last several decades has focused on reshaping lists of what to "cover" and using high stakes summative assessments to measure the memory of facts. The curriculum-driven instructional model has generally gone unchallenged for over 150 years. But the age in which we live offers us the option to change.

> **This is the age of transformation, unleashing the potential of men and women of every race and in every corner of the world, unleashing the power of technology and science, unleashing the power of learning.**

Our challenges are great, but our awareness, knowledge, skills and technology have never been greater. **Our capacity for change has never been greater.** We can transcend the limitations of an education process **that punishes the poor** and fails to teach most students to develop the skills, habits, and character needed in the modern world.

Somewhere in Mississippi a first grader receives reading instruction. His teacher knows exactly which skills he has already developed, and how to design instruction at just the right level of difficulty to keep him fully engaged. He loves school, and he loves learning.

In New Hampshire a tenth grader has been slacking off in science. Just a few years ago she might have earned a C and moved along, but her teachers don't do it that way anymore. She asks her teacher for a meeting, and they put together a plan for her to catch up on some of the science outcomes for which she has not yet developed competency.

A ten-year-old homeschooled student has fallen in love with math. After developing the essential early math skills using lots of hands on activities, she started to work using a digital math learning program. She's way ahead of age expectations, and goes back and forth between her digital learning program, the Khan Academy, evening sessions with Dad, and her on-line support team to find challenges that are interesting.

In his second year of college, a young man has completed all but a few of the requirements for his bachelor's degree, along with three certificates of skill. Many of his credits were earned using a competency based program in his high school and local community college. This semester he's preparing his resume and applying for jobs, and with his competency profile he is able to show prospective employers exactly which skills he has developed and is ready to use in the workplace.

A graduate level education student is reviewing her personal vision statement to help her develop a personal learning plan. After eight years of teaching she has a more mature view of what she can really accomplish. Soon she'll sit with a program planner, who will add this student's personal learning goals to the competency expectations for her advanced degree. Then they'll plan a learning program that supports the development of competency for every objective.

The **transformation has begun.** Learning and persistence are the currency of the future. Our children, and students of any age, deserve a thoughtful education system which recognizes individual learning readiness, and offers a clear pathway to the knowledge and skills they need.

# Appendix 1: Organizational Self-Assessment for Readiness to Implement Competency Based Learning

Please reflect on the following statements, indicating how accurate this statement is for your organization. Rate 1 for low accuracy and up to 5 for high accuracy. Circle your response.

1_2_3_4_5 We have taken the time to study competency based learning and how it applies to our learning programs.

1_2_3_4_5 A leadership team comprised of committed school and community members has been identified.

1_2_3_4_5 A point of beginning for competency based learning has been identified.

1_2_3_4_5 A clear vision for where we hope to be in three to five years has been developed.

1_2_3_4_5 A comprehensive transition plan has been established.

1_2_3_4_5 Staff, administration, student, and community training needs have been identified.

1_2_3_4_5 Obstacles to implementation have been identified and considered.

1_2_3_4_5 Necessary resources to support transition activities are in place.

1_2_3_4_5 Our vision and first steps in transition are clear to all concerned.

# Appendix 2: Resources for the Further Study of Competency Based Learning

**Achieve** is an independent, nonpartisan, nonprofit education reform organization working with states to raise academic standards and graduation requirements, improve assessments, and strengthen accountability. http://www.achieve.org/publications/advancing-competency-based-pathways-college-and-career-readiness

**American Youth Policy Forum** provides learning opportunities toward the development of effective youth and education policies. Their guiding principles include Student-Centered Learning, Advancement upon Mastery, Multiple Pathways to Success, and Creating Collaborative Systems that Support Youth. http://www.aypf.org

**Annie E. Casey Foundation** is a private charitable organization dedicated to helping build better futures for disadvantaged children in the U.S. Their work focuses on strengthening families, building stronger communities, and education issues. They have been strong advocates for the importance of Preschool through Grade 3 learning outcomes. http://www.aecf.org

**Aurora Institute** provides a variety of resources to help you understand competency education, including examples, policy, practice tips, and CompetencyWorks Issue Briefs.
https://aurora-institute.org
https://aurora-institute.org/our-work/competencyworks

**Carnegie Foundation for the Advancement of Teaching** is a U.S.-based education policy and research center. It has offered conducted research on the efficacy of the practice of Carnegie

Units and seat time to measure learning. http://www.carnegie foundation.org/?s=competency+based&submit=go

**Council for Adult & Experiential Learning** is a nonprofit that works within the higher education, public, and private sectors to help adult learners get the education and training they need. With funding from Lumina Foundation for Education, the Council for Adult and Experiential Learning (CAEL) offers postsecondary institutions training on competency-based education. http://www.cael.org/what-we-do/competency-based-education

**Chugach School District, Alaska.**
http://www.chugachschools.com/pages/Chugach_School_District

http://www.competencyworks.org/resources/how-alaskas-chugach-district-changed-education-through-performance-based-learning/

**Clayton Christensen Institute for Disruptive Innovation** is a nonprofit, nonpartisan think tank dedicated to improving the world through disruptive innovation. The theory of disruptive innovation describes a process by which a product or service transforms an existing market by introducing simplicity, convenience, accessibility, and affordability. http://www.christenseninstitute.org/our-mission/#sthash.YRRfWSZD.dpuf
http://www.christenseninstitute.org/

**Competency-Based Education Network** (C-BEN), administered by Public Agenda, is a group of regionally accredited colleges and universities working together to address shared challenges to designing, developing, and scaling competency-based degree programs. http://www.cael.org/what-we-do/competency-based-education#sthash.gklbqi3e.dpuf

**Council of Chief State School Officers** is a nonpartisan, nonprofit organization of public officials who head departments of elementary and secondary education. Their Innovation Lab Network is a group of states taking action to test and implement student-centered approaches to learning that will transform public education. http://www.ccsso.org/What_We_Do/Innovation_Lab_Network.html#sthash.abW0NRhI.dpuf

**Early Learning Foundation** offers training and support for school districts and parent organizations regarding competency based learning in the preschool to grade three years. Its Early Learning Success Initiative manages use of the *Essential Skill Inventories, PreK to Grade 3*, a competency based framework for measuring on-going progress toward essential skills in all the domains of early childhood. http://earlylearningfoundation.com

**International Association for K-12 Online Learning** (iNACOL) supports the development and use of online, blended, and competency-based learning models to achieve personalized and competency-based learning, and offers a variety of reports and webinars. http://www.inacol.org/AK-12 Federal Policy Framework for Competency Education: Building Capacity for SystemsChange

**Jobs for the Future.** JFF works with public and private partners across the country to design and expand models that: build basic skills, improve high school instruction, increase graduation rates, increase college entry, and provide support to help college students and job trainees. http://www.jff.org/publications

**KnowledgeWorks** is a social enterprise focused on ensuring that students experience meaningful personalized learning which supports success in college, career and civic life. www.knowledgeworks.org

**Lumina Foundation for Education** is a private, Indianapolis-based foundation. Its mission is to expand student access to and success in education beyond high school. It has sponsored a series of reports on competency based higher education. http://www.luminafoundation.org/resources
http://www.luminafoundation.org/files/resources/competency-based-education-landscape.pdf

**National Assessment of Educational Progress** is the largest continuing and nationally representative assessment of what American students know and can do in core subjects. NAEP is a congressionally mandated project administered by the National Center for Education Statistics (NCES), within the Institute of Education Sciences (IES) of the U.S. Department of Education. http://nces.ed.gov/nationsreportcard

**National Association of Elementary School Principals** is a professional organization serving elementary and middle school principals and other education leaders throughout the United States, Canada, and overseas. It has developed a competency framework for effective principals working with the early childhood years. *Leading Pre-K-3 Learning Communities: Competencies for Effective Principal Practice.* https://www.naesp.org/sites/default/files/leading-pre-k-3-learning-communities-executive-summary.pdf

**National Center for Competency-Based Learning** (NCCBL) is a New Hampshire based 501(c)(3) nonprofit charitable organization founded in 2013. http://www.nccbl.org/aboutus.html

**Nellie Mae Education Foundation** works with schools in New England to implement the principles of student-centered learning that is personalized, engaging, and competency-based. They offer a rich library of publications which support competency based learning options. http://www.nmefoundation.org/resources

**New Hampshire Department of Education** has been a leader in state competency based learning initiatives. The NHDoE has established model Literacy, Mathematics, Science, Work-Study, and Arts competencies for high school graduation. http://education.nh.gov/innovations/hs_redesign/competencies.htm
http://education.nh.gov/innovations/hs_redesign

**Organisation for Economic Co-operation and Development (OECD)** is the sponsoring agency for the Programme for International Student Assessment (PISA). This triennial international survey evaluates education systems worldwide by testing the skills and knowledge of 15-year-old students. In 2012 Around 510,000 students in 65 economies took part in the PISA 2012 assessment of reading, mathematics and science representing about 28 million 15-year-olds globally. PISA is an ongoing triennial survey, allowing countries participating in successive surveys to compare their students' performance over time and assess the impact of education policy decisions. http://www.oecd.org/pisa/keyfindings/pisa-2012-results.htm http://www.oecd.org

**Rand Corporation** is a research organization, working with nations around the world on issues including security, health, education, sustainability, growth, and development. Rand Education's research projects include competency based education. http://www.rand.org/education/projects/competency-based-education.html

**Re-inventing Schools Coalition (RISC)** is a division of Marzano Research. It was established by core members of the team at Chugach School District, and offers training and support materials to school districts. The history of RISC is described in *Delivering on the Promise: The Education Revolution*, by DeLorenzo, Battino, Schreiber, and Gaddy-Carrio. http://www.reinventingschools.org

# Study Guide

Chapter 1: Someday Soon (A Fable)

1. Describe a learning experience in which you remember being fully engaged in the learning process, challenged but not overwhelmed.
2. Describe a learning experience in which you remember being frustrated and overwhelmed by the work or presentation.
3. Write a fable that describes the learning life of a disadvantaged student within a typical modern school.

Chapter 2: Informed Instruction Leads to Competency, Part One

1. Describe a situation in which you were careful to use informed instruction with your own child.
2. What are some of the professions that have relied upon competency based learning systems for many years? Explain why that happened.
3. What happens when the pace of instruction does not match the readiness level of a student?

Chapter 3: The Curriculum-Driven Model: A Brief History

1. During the late 19th and early 20th century, public school systems developed using a standard curriculum. Explain how standard delivery of instruction met the needs of society in the early 1900s, but fails to meet the needs of modern learners.
2. What vestiges of Horace Mann and Frederick Winslow Taylor can be seen in recent iterations of federal and state education policy?

3. Why have successful modern businesses moved away from one-size-fits-all learning and "the one best way" model of management?

## Chapter 4: Without Learning Competency There Can Be No Equity

1. In what way did the standard delivery of instruction lead to the sorting of successful and non-successful students?
2. How did society's need for an informed and literate population in 1900 differ from the needs of today?
3. In what way has the pressure of standardized testing in the last few decades influenced our use of standardized delivery of content?
4. In what ways has being a successful learner, and developing the capacity for intrinsically motivated learning, never been more crucial for the financial and social future of our children?
5. Describe, in your opinion, some of the conspicuous failures caused by our continued use of the curriculum-driven model of instruction?
6. In what ways are disadvantaged students especially affected by the curriculum-driven instructional model?

## Chapter 5: Giving Up Unproductive Mental Models

1. Quantity of content, grading on the curve, and sorting good and poor students. Among these three, in your opinion which idea has caused the greatest harm to students? Why?
2. Some parents just want to know that their child is doing better than other children. To this parent, how would you describe the need for competency based learning?
3. Fifty years ago, the United States was generally considered to have the best educated workforce in the world. How did we lose that advantage?

Chapter 6: Building a New Model

1. Describe a situation in which someone personalized instruction for you.
2. Describe a situation in which you personalized instruction for a child or student.
3. In what way do quality digital learning systems match instruction to the needs and readiness of students?
4. Describe a real situation in which a company uses personalized instruction to train employees in crucial tasks.
5. Respond to this statement by the Oregon Education Roundtable: *In a proficiency system, failure or poor performance may be part of the student's learning curve, but it is not an outcome.*

Chapter 7: Principles of Instruction Leading to Competency

1. Rewrite the *Principles of Instruction Leading to Competency* in your own words.
2. Why is understanding the instructional level needs of each child an important condition for competency based learning?
3. Identifying a small set of crucial learning outcomes is different than making a list of all the content we hope to "cover" in a course of study. Explain the difference.
4. Is it fair to let some students have more time to learn the content?
5. Is it fair to let some students move on to more advanced content when they are ready?

Chapter 8: Teaching Differently

1. Describe some important teacher behaviors which suffer in a content-driven instruction system?
2. What professional development needs must be considered as we begin to develop competency based learning systems?

3. Should high school credits be given for learning that is accomplished on the job, at home, independently, or anywhere outside the school?
4. Should college credits be given for learning that is accomplished on the job, at home, independently, or anywhere else outside the structure of a course?
5. How might the role of the parents change in a competency based learning system?
6. Describe the characteristics of men and women who will thrive as teachers within a competency based learning model.

Chapter 9: Systems Thinking for Competency Based Learning

1. A successful competency based learning experience starts with the identification of clear learning goals. Why?
2. Are the skills needed to earn a tech certificate, pilot's license, or professional medical license clear? Contrast this with the experience of taking most high school or college courses.
3. A 3rd grade student is given a C on his report card. What specific information about his progress toward becoming a successful reader does this grade offer?
4. In what way do good coaches use clear learning goals?
5. If you are teaching a child to throw and catch, but the child is struggling to successfully catch the small ball, what innovations might you consider?
6. A student is struggling to solve two-digit subtraction problems that require borrowing.
   a. Upon analysis you find that he does not have full proficiency for recognizing number groups (to 10), or solving combination problems (to 20) using manipulatives. What do you do with this information?
7. In a digital math program, a student scores 78% correct on a review assessment. What does the digital program do with this information?

8. Describe a learning program you have used which carefully monitors your progress and adapts to meet your needs.
9. What do you see as the greatest innovation opportunities for thoughtful educators as we move toward competency based learning?

Chapter 10: Whole Child Competency

1. How has our recent history of content-driven instruction and high-stakes testing impacted the development of intrinsic motivation among our students?
2. Self-regulation begins with the development of self-calming, focusing, persisting, delaying gratification, and adjusting your emotional, physical, and attentional state to meet the needs of your situation. How does the capacity for self-regulation impact a student's opportunity for success in school?
3. What activities or routines at school support the development of self-regulation?
4. What activities or routines at home support the development of self-regulation?
5. How will intrinsic motivation impact a student's success within a competency based learning system?
6. What contributes to a learning environment in which students may feel highly anxious or insecure?
7. What contributes to an environment in which educators may also feel high anxious or insecure?
8. Could self-regulation and social-emotional skills be developed using a competency based model? Explain.
9. Describe a classroom in which kids learn to be calm and focused, and to work well with other.
10. Describe a school environment which prioritizes the development of self-regulation, intrinsic motivation, and social-emotional skills.

Chapter 11: Creating the Culture of a Learning Organization

1. How would you describe the organizational culture of your school or district?
2. *For decades, state and district education officials have set the expectations for what should be taught, in what order, and at what age. In recent years politicians and bureaucrats have further dictated when and how this content will be tested, how schools will be graded, and how teachers will be evaluated. We are in the strong arms of a top- down Taylorian approach to every aspect of managing public education.* Please respond.
3. Is your school or district ready for the professional learning demands of competency based system?
4. In what way could your school or district begin to prepare for the transition to competency based learning?

Chapter 12: Learning for Understanding and Application

1. Young children are wired to learn. They are curious, engaged, and alive to learning.
   How does the experience of school affect this condition for most children? Why?
2. For intrinsic motivation to learn, why is it vital that learning goals be clear?
3. For intrinsic motivation to learn, why is it vital that learning goals be attainable?
4. For intrinsic motivation to learn, why is it vital that learning goals be personally meaningful?
5. How could choice be included into a competency based learning system?

Chapter 13: Masters of the Trade: Game Designers

1. While playing your favorite digital game (if you have one), in what ways do the game designers keep you engaged?

2. How does differentiated instruction at school use some of the learning concepts and principles demonstrated in high quality digital games?
3. How does blended instruction at school use some of the learning concepts and principles demonstrated in high quality digital games?
4. How does project based instruction at school use some of the learning concepts and principles demonstrated in high quality digital games?
5. Why don't game designers give grades to a player after each session?
6. How effectively do typical schools help a student develop an identity as a successful learner?

## Chapter 14: What's Happening in Competency Based Learning Initiatives

1. Research one state's competency initiative. What motivated the initiative? What were the first few steps in the process? What were the challenges they encountered?
2. States are approaching competency in many different ways. What factors are likely to influence the development of a competency based learning initiative in your state?
3. What are the challenges to consider when creating a definition of skills and knowledge needed for college and career readiness?
4. Are credit requirements for high school and college graduation an antiquated notion which no longer serves any purpose?
5. Should all students meet the exact same standards for high school graduation, or could personalized learning programs lead to different sets of meaningful skills?
6. How might competency based learning systems be applied to the early childhood years to improve learning outcomes for disadvantaged students?
7. Identify one competency based learning model for higher education within your state.

a. Why was this developed, and how effectively do they ensure quality learning outcomes?
8. Why have medical and technical training programs long relied upon a competency based model?
9. Describe procedures for a primarily on-line IHE which would allow it to achieve level 5 status as a competency based learning system.
10. What are some of the challenges to a university considering moving toward competency based learning?
11. How could a professional education association contribute to the development of competency based learning systems for their members?
12. Choose one on-line university or training program, and evaluate its system using the rubric for considering the quality of an IHE competency based learning initiative.
13. In your opinion, is the use of Carnegie Units and credits for high school graduation an antiquated notion whose time has passed? Explain.
14. How do the intended purposes of the *European Framework of Key Competences for Lifelong Learning* (2007) contrast to the intended purposes of the Common Core State Standards (2010).
15. What are the challenges to establishing state competency standards for high school graduation?
16. Imagine a high school which operates on a competency standards framework, and has abandoned the credit requirement system. How would it function differently than typical high schools today?
17. In your district or community, what are the crucial outcomes which will help young men and women become ready to live and work in our changing world?
18. Why do third grade learning skills serve as such an important predictor of long-term learning success?
19. Is it possible to establish competency standards for language, phonologic skills, literacy, numeracy, motor skills, social-emotional skills and self-regulation skills in the early learning years? What are the challenges?

20. How can parents participate in an early childhood competency based learning initiative?
21. Describe the relationship between formative and summative assessment in a successful early learning CBL initiative.
22. In your view, could digital learning systems ever replace interactive physical and social learning during the early childhood years?

## Chapter 15: Teacher Education: Building Pathways to Skills That Matter

1. How well did the teacher education or administrative education you experienced match the expectations of a high quality competency based learning system?
2. What do you really think about the efficacy of the CEU system in your state?
3. Review one set of recommendations for teaching or administrative competency.
   Summarize and evaluate.
4. Develop a set of recommendations for teaching competency. These competencies could apply to a single discipline at one grade level, or to a level of instruction (early childhood, upper elementary, middle school, high school), or to any other segment of teaching.
   What are the specific skills that would allow teachers to demonstrate a high standard of competency?
5. Teacher competency matters. Explain.

## Chapter 16: Distracted by the Debate Over What to Cover

1. Do the Common Core State Standards represent one more attempt to describe the "one best way" of one-size-fits-all instruction? Explain.
2. In what ways has the introduction of CCSS and national testing systems impacted the lives of children in your school, or your life as a teacher?

3. Describe three topics for professional learning you would love to see vigorously pursued in your school or district? What has prevented this professional learning from being considered in recent years?

## Chapter 17: Letting Go of Curriculum-Driven Instruction

1. Among the teachers and administrators you know well, what factors are likely to make the change to competency based learning difficult?
2. Describe a teacher you know who has used a similar course curriculum and/or set of lesson plans for many years. How will this teacher respond to the proposal to transition to a competency based learning system?
3. Is anyone in your district or institution of learning already using a competency based learning structure? If so, please describe.

## Chapter 18: Transitioning from Curriculum-Driven to Competency Based Learning

1. In your schools, what is the point of beginning you would choose for competency based learning?
2. Who are the thinkers and leaders who will join you in the process of transforming toward competency based learning?
3. Describe one of the essential early steps in your transition plan, and how you can support that step.

## Chapter 19: Informed Instruction Leads to Competency, Part Two

1. Compare and contrast the underlying premises of the curriculum-driven instructional model with competency based learning.
2. What is your definition of informed instruction?
3. Describe your personal connection to the work of building competency based learning systems.

## Chapter 20: The Spirit of Transformation

1. *Those of us who are educators, parents, and community leaders have the information, tools, and opportunity to create an educational process which works for many more students, a process which respects diversity, embraces personalization, and continuously improves.* Please respond.
2. What role will you choose in the transformation to competency based learning?

# References

ACT (2013). The Reality of College Readiness. http://www.act.org/readinessreality/13/pdf/Reality-of-College-Readiness-2013.pdf

Alberta Education (2011). *Framework for Student Learning: Competencies for Engaged Thinkers and Ethical Citizens with an Entrepreneurial Spirit.* http://education.alberta.ca/media/6581166/framework.pdf

Ames, C. (1992). Classrooms: Goals, structures, and student motivation. *Journal of Educational Psychology, 84*(3), 261–271.

Annie E. Casey Foundation (2010). *Early warning! Why reading by the end of third grade matters.* Baltimore, MD: Annie E. Casey Foundation.

Annie E. Casey Foundation (2014). Why Inequality Hurts Kids and Families, retrieved from http://www.aecf.org/blog/why-inequality-hurts-kids-and-families/

Betts, E. A. (1946). *Foundations of reading instruction with emphasis on differentiated guidance.* New York, NY: American Book Company.

British Columbia Ministry of Education (2013). *Exploring Curriculum Design, Transforming Curriculum and Assessment.* https://www.bced.gov.bc.ca/irp/docs/exp_curr_design.pdf

British Columbia Ministry of Education update (2015). *British Columbia Education Plan.* http://www.bcedplan.ca/

Burns, M. K. (2007). Reading at the instructional level with children identified as learning disabled: Potential implications for response to intervention. *School Psychology Quarterly, 22*(3), 297–313.

Buros Center for Testing (1990). *Standards for Teacher Competence in Educational Assessment of Students.* http://buros.org/standards-teacher-competence-educational-assessment-students

Colorado Dept. of Education (2013). *Colorado's Graduation Guidelines: 2013 & Beyond.* http://www.cde.state.co.us/postsecondary/graduationguidelinesworkgroupwebinar

Council of Chief State School Officers (CCSSO) Interstate Teacher Assessment and Support Consortium (2013). *Model Core Teaching Standards and Learning Progressions for Teachers 1.0.* http://www.ccsso.org/Resources/Publications/InTASC_Model_Core_Teaching_Standards_2011_MS_Word_Version.html

CompetencyWorks Wiki (2018). *Detailed Definition of Competency Based Education.* http://competencyworks.pbworks.com/w/page/67945372/Detailed%20Definition%20of%20Competency%20Education

Csikszentmihalyi, M. (1985). Emergent motivation and the evolution of the self. In D. A. Kleiber & M. Maehr (Eds.), *Advances in motivation and achievement (Vol. 4,* pp. 93–119). Greenwich, CT: JAI Press.

DeLorenzo, R., Battino, W., Schreiber, R., & Gaddy-Carrio, B. (2008). *Delivering on the promise.* Bloomington, IN: Solution Tree.

Dempster, F. N. (1993). Exposing our students to less should help them learn. *Phi Delta Kappan, 74*(6), 432–437.

Downs, R. B. (1974). *Horace Mann: Champion of the public schools.* Woodbridge, CT: Twayne Publishers.

Driscoll, M. P. (1994). *Psychology of learning for instruction.* MA: Paramount Publishing.

Duckworth, A. L., Peterson, C., Matthews, M. D., & Kelly, D. R. (2007). Grit: Perseverance and passion for long-term goals. *Journal of Personality and Social Psychology, 92*(6), 1087–1101. 10.1037/0022-3514.92.6.1087

DuFour, R., DuFour, R. et al. (2016) *Learning by doing: A handbook for professional learning communities at work.* Bloomington, IN: Solution Tree.

DuFour, R., & Eaker, R. (1998). *Professional learning communities at work: Best practices for enhancing student achievement.* Bloomington, IN: Solution Tree (formerly National Educational Service).

EPE Research Center (2010). http://www.edweek.org/media/34gradrate-c1.pdf.

European Commission (2007). *Key competences for lifelong learning.* European Reference Framework Luxembourg: Office for Official Publications of the European Communities. http://eurlex.europa.eu/LexUriServ/LexUriServ.do?uri=OJ:L:2006:394:0010:0018:EN:PDF

Fielding, L., Kerr, N., & Rosier, P. (2007). *Annual growth for all students, catch up growth for those who are behind.* Kennewick, WA: The New Foundation Press.

*Fourth grade mathematics achievement levels | KIDS COUNT Data Center.* (2019). The Annie E. Casey Foundation, https://datacenter.kidscount.org/data/line/5116-fourth-grade-readingachievementlevels/share/loc=1~loct=1/1~any~false~1729,871,573,36,867,38,18,16,14,13~asc~1185,1186,1187,1188~11560#1/any/false/1729,871,573,36,867,38,18,16,14,13/asc/1185,1186,1187,1188/11560

*Fourth grade reading achievement levels | KIDS COUNT Data Center.* (2019). The Annie E. Casey Foundation, https://datacenter.kidscount.org/data/line/5116-fourth-grade-reading-achievementlevels/share/loc=1~loct=1/1~any~false~1729,871,573,36,867,38,18,16,14,13~asc~1185,1186,1187,1188~11560#1/any/false/1729,871,573,36,867,38,18,16,14,13/asc/1185,1186,1187,1188/11560

Fuchs, L., & Fuchs, D. (1988). Curriculum-based measurement. A methodology for evaluating and improving student programs. *Assessment for Effective Intervention, 14*(1), 3–13.

Fullan, M., & Hargreaves, A. (1996). *What's worth fighting for in your school?* New York: Teachers College Press.

Gickling, E. E., & Armstrong, D. L. (1978). Levels of instructional difficulty as related to on- task behavior, task completion, and comprehension. *Journal of Learning Disabilities, 11*(9), 559–566. https://doi.org/10.1177/002221947801100905

Goodman, M.J., Sands, A.M., & Coley, R.J. (2015). *America's Skills Challenge: Millennials and the Future.* Princeton, NJ: Educational Testing Service.

Hattie, J. (2009). *Visible learning.* Routledge Press.

Hernandez, D. (2011). *Double Jeopardy: How third-grade reading skills and poverty influence high school graduation.* Baltimore, MD: Annie E. Casey Foundation. http://www.cde.state.co.us/SecondaryInitiatives/GraduationGuidelines.htm

(iNACOL) International Association for K-12 Online Learning (2014). *iNACOL Blended Learning Teacher Competency Framework.* https://www.inacol.org/wp-content/uploads/2014/10/iNACOL-Blended-Learning-Teacher-Competency-Framework.pdf

Kanigel, R. (1997). *The one best way: Frederick Winslow Taylor and the Enigma of efficiency.* New York: Viking.

Laitinen, A. (2012). *Cracking the credit hour*. New America Foundation. https://www.newamerica.org/education-policy/cracking-the-credit-hour/

Lepper, M. R., & Hodell, M. (1989). Intrinsic motivation in the classroom. In C. Ames & R. Ames (Eds.), *Research on motivation in education* (Vol. 3, pp. 73–105). San Diego: Academic Press.

Long, H., Fowers, A., & Dam, A. V. (2021). Why America has 8.4 million unemployed when there are 10 million job openings. *Washington Post*. https://www.washingtonpost.com/business/2021/09/04/ten-million-job-openings-labor-shortage/

Longley, R. (2021). *Up to 75 percent of US youth ineligible for military service*. ThoughtCo. https://www.thoughtco.com/us-youth-ineligible-for-military-service-3322428

Maine Department of Education (2012). *Education evolving: Maine's Plan for Putting Learners First*. http://maine.gov/doe/plan

Marzano, R. J. (2003). *What works in schools: Translating research into action*. Alexandria, VA: Association for Supervision and Curriculum Development

Marzano, R. J. (2006). Wayne County RESA presentation PowerPoint slide.

Mayer, R. (2002). Rote Versus Meaningful Learning. *Theory Into Practice*, 41(4), 226–232.

Mischel, W., Shoda, Y., & Rodriguez, M. (1989). Delay of gratification in children. *Science*, 244(4907), 933–938.

Mission Readiness (2009). *Ready Willing and Unable to Serve*, a Report Prepared for the Joint Chiefs of Staff. http://cdn.missionreadiness.org/NATEE1109.pdf

Moffitt T. E., Arseneault, L., Belsky, D., Dickson, N., Hancox, R. J., Harrington, H., Houts, R., Poulton, R., Roberts, B. W., Ross, S., Sears, M. R., Thomson, W. M., Caspi, A. (2011). A Gradient of Childhood Self-Control Predicts Health, Wealth, and Public Safety. *Proceedings of the National Academy of Sciences of the United States of America*, 108(7), 2693–2698. http://www.ncbi.nlm.nih.gov/pmc/articles/PMC3041102/

NAEP 12th-Grade Achievement Levels (2015). *Race and Ethnicity in Higher Education*. https://www.equityinhighered.org/indicators/secondary-school-completion/naep-12th-grade-achievement-levels/

NAEP Mathematics: National Achievement-Level Results (2019). NAEP Report Card: Mathematics. https://www.nationsreportcard.gov/mathematics/nation/achievement/?grade=12

NAEP Reading: National Achievement-Level Results (2019). NAEP Report Card: Reading. https://www.nationsreportcard.gov/reading/nation/achievement/?grade=12

National Association for Elementary School Principals (2014). *Leading Pre-K-3 Learning Communities: Competencies for Effective Principal Practice.* https://www.naesp.org/sites/default/files/leading-pre-k-3-learning-communities-executive-summary.pdf

National Center for Education Statistics (2014). U.S. Department of Education, Common Core of Data (CCD), "NCES Common Core of Data State Dropout and Graduation Rate Data file," School Year 2010–11, Provisional Version 1a.

National Center for Education Statistics (2019). *The NCES Fast Facts Tool provides quick answers to many education questions.* https://nces.ed.gov/fastfacts/display.asp?id=40

National Center for Education Statistics (2020). *Digest of Education Statistics.* NCES #2022009. Washington D.C.: US Department of Education.

National Mathematics Advisory Council (2008). *Foundations for Success: The final report of the national mathematics advisory council.* Washington D.C.: US Department of Education.

National Technical Information Service (1991). *Secretary's commission on achieving necessary skills (SCANS).* Washington DC: U.S. Department of Labor, NTIS Order Number: PB92- 146711INZ.

New Hampshire DOE (2007). *New Hampshire's Vision for Redesign, Moving from High Schools to Learning Communities.* http://education.nh.gov/innovations/hs_redesign/documents/vision.pdf

New Hampshire DOE (2014). *Minimum Standards for Public School Approval.* http://education.nh.gov/legislation/documents/ed3062014-min-stands.pdf

New Hampshire English Language Arts Competencies (2013). New Hampshire State Board of Education. http://education.nh.gov/competencies/documents/ela-competencies.pdf

New Hampshire K-12 Science Competencies (2014). New Hampshire State Board of Education. http://education.nh.gov/innovations/hs_redesign/documents/ccrs-competencies-science.pdf

New Hampshire Mathematics Competencies (2013). New Hampshire State Board of Education. http://education.nh.gov/competencies/documents/NHSBEApprovedMathFinal2.20.13.pdf

Oregon Education Roundtable (2009). *Proficiency Based Learning*, http://theworldlink.com/news/local/education/oregon-education-roundtable---proficiency-based-instruction-and-assessment/pdf_35e52372-2d1a-11e3-bdc3-001a4bcf887a.html

*Program for International Student Assessment (PISA) – Trends in Student Performance: Trends in U.S. Performance.* (2015). National Center for Education Statistics. https://nces.ed.gov/surveys/pisa/pisa2015/pisa2015highlights_6.asp

Redden, E. (2020, February 18). 41% of Recent Grads Work in Jobs Not Requiring a Degree. Inside Higher Ed. https://www.insidehighered.com/quicktakes/2020/02/18/41-recent-grads-work-jobs-not-requiring-degree

Schmidt, W. H., & Cogan, L. S. (2009). The Myth of Equal Content. *Educational Leadership*, 67(3), 44–47, Alexandria, VA: ASCD.

Schmidt, W. H., McKnight, C. C., & Raizen, S. A. (1996). *Splintered vision: An investigation of U.S. science and mathematics education: Executive summary.* Lansing, MI: U.S. National Research Center for the Third International Mathematics and Science Study, Michigan State University.

Schmidt, W. H., McKnight, C. C., Houang, R. T., Wang, H. C., Wiley, D. E., Cogan, L. S. & Wolfe, R. G. (2001). *Why schools matter: A cross-national comparison of curriculum and learning.* San Francisco, CA: Jossey-Bass.

Schmidt, W. H., Wang, H. A., & McKnight, C. C. (2005). Curriculum coherence: An examination of U.S. mathematics and science content standards from an international perspective. *Journal of Curriculum Studies*, 37(5), 525–529.

Schmoker, M. & Marzano, R. (1999). Realizing the promise of standards-based education. *Education Leadership*, 56(6), Alexandria, VA: ASCD, 17–21.

Serino, L. (2017, April 7). What international test scores reveal about American education. *Brookings*. https://www.brookings.edu/blog/brown-center-chalkboard/2017/04/07/what-international-test-scores-reveal-about-american-education/

Snow, C. E., Burns, S., & Griffin, P.(Eds.) (1998). *Preventing reading difficulties in young children, report of the committee on the prevention of reading difficulties in young children.* Washington, DC: National Academy Press.

Sornson, B. (2012). *Fanatically formative: Successful learning during the crucial K-3 years.* Thousand Oaks, CA: Corwin Press.

Sornson, B. (2012). *Essential skills inventories PK-3.* Brighton, MI: Early Learning Foundation.

Sornson, B. (2014). *Essential math skills.* Huntington Beach, CA: Shell Education.

Sornson, B. (2014). *Essential math skills inventory, PK to grade 3.* Brighton, MI: Early Learning Foundation.

Sornson, B. (2015). The Effects of Using the Essential Skills Inventory on Teacher Perception of High-Quality Classroom Instruction. *Preventing School Failure: Alternative Education for Children and Youth, 59*(3), 161–167.

Sornson, B. & Davis, D. (2013). Focus on Essential Learning Outcomes. *Journal of Research Initiatives, 1*(1), Article 8, 54–59. http://digitalcommons.uncfsu.edu/jri/vol1/iss1/8

Spoehr, T. (2018). *The Looming National Security Crisis: Young Americans Unable to Serve in the Military.* The Heritage Foundation. https://www.heritage.org/defense/report/the-looming-national-security-crisis-young-americans-unable-serve-the-military

State of Vermont Board of Education (2013). *Vermont Education Quality Standards.* http://education.vermont.gov/documents/EDU_EQS_01_23_14_Proposed_Final_Rule.pdf

Stiggins, R. (1999). Assessment, student confidence, and school success. *Phi Delta Kappan, 81*(3), 191–198.

Strong, K. (2019). *Young people mostly unqualified for military service and careers* [York Daily Record]. https://www.usatoday.com/story/news/nation/2019/05/14/military-service-most-young-people-dont-qualify-careers/3665840002/

Taylor, B. P. (2010). *Horace Mann's troubling legacy: The education of democratic citizens.* Lawrence, KS: University Press of Kansas.

Taylor, F. (1911). *The principles of scientific management.* New York and London: Harper & Brothers.

Teacher Leadership Consortium (2014). *Teacher Leader Model Standards.* https://www.ets.org/s/education_topics/teaching_quality/pdf/teacher_leader_model_standards.pdf

The Council of Chief State School Officers (2015). *Innovation in Action: State Pathways for Advancing Student-Centered Learning.* http://www.ccsso.org/Documents/ILN%20Logic%20Model%20White%20Paper-online%20file.pdf

Torgesen, J. K. (2002). The prevention of reading difficulties. *Journal of School Psychology, 40,* 7–26.

Torgesen, J. K. (1998). Catch them before they Fail. *American Educator, 22*(1–2), 32–39.

U.S. Census Bureau (2014). Educational Attainment in the United States: 2013, Retrieved March 26, 2014.

U.S. Census Bureau (2014). Historical Income Tables: Income Inequality. http://www.census.gov/hhes/www/income/data/historical/inequality/

U.S. Department of Education (2010). *National Education Technology Plan.* http://tech.ed.gov/netp/

United Nations Educational, Scientific and Cultural Organization (2008). *ICT Competency Standards for Teachers, Implementation Guidelines.* http://unesdoc.unesco.org/images/0015/001562/156209E.pdf

Vermont Quality Education Standards (2013). https://education.vermont.gov/education-quality-assurance/education-quality-standards

Vygotsky, L. S. (1978). *Mind in society: The development of higher psychological processes.* Cambridge, MA: Harvard University Press.

Walser, N. (2021, August 16). Emerging from the pandemic, districts look to expand personalized competency-based education. The Washington Post. Retrieved April 27, 2022, from https://www.washingtonpost.com/local/education/schools-competency-based-education/2021/08/13/a8faac98-fac0-11eb-9c0e-97e29906a970_story.html

World Inequality Lab (2022). *World Inequality Report 2022,* https://wir2022.wid.world/

For Product Safety Concerns and Information please contact our EU representative GPSR@taylorandfrancis.com
Taylor & Francis Verlag GmbH, Kaufingerstraße 24, 80331 München, Germany

www.ingramcontent.com/pod-product-compliance
Lightning Source LLC
Chambersburg PA
CBHW051116230426
43667CB00014B/2610